Prejudice and Discrimination

INQUIRY INTO CRUCIAL AMERICAN PROBLEMS

Series Editor · JACK R. FRAENKEL

Prejudice and Discrimination:

Can We Eliminate Them?

FRED R. HOLMES

Chairman, Social Studies Department
Burlingame High School
Burlingame, California

PRENTICE-HALL, INC. ENGLEWOOD CLIFFS, N.J.

Titles in this series:

CRIME AND CRIMINALS: What Should We Do About Them?
Jack R. Fraenkel

PREJUDICE AND DISCRIMINATION: Can We Eliminate Them?
Fred R. Holmes

THE DRUG SCENE: Help or Hang-up?
Walter L. Way

POVERTY IN AN AFFLUENT SOCIETY: Personal Problem or National Disgrace?
David A. Durfee

COUNTRY, CONSCIENCE, AND CONSCRIPTION: Can They Be Reconciled?
Leo A. Bressler and Marion A. Bressler

VOICES OF DISSENT: Positive Good or Disruptive Evil?
Frank Kane

CITIES IN CRISIS: Decay or Renewal?
Rudie W. Tretten

TEEN-AGERS AND SEX: Revolution or Reaction?
Jack L. Nelson

PROPAGANDA, POLLS, AND PUBLIC OPINION: Are the People Manipulated?
Malcolm G. Mitchell

ALIENATION: Individual or Social Problem?
Ronald V. Urick

EDUCATION AND OPPORTUNITY: For What and For Whom?
Gordon M. Seely

FOREIGN POLICY: Intervention, Involvement, or Isolation?
Alvin Wolf

Prentice-Hall International, Inc.,
London
Prentice-Hall of Australia, Pty. Ltd.,
Sydney
Prentice-Hall of Canada, Ltd.,
Toronto
Prentice-Hall of India Private Ltd.,
New Delhi
Prentice-Hall of Japan, Inc.,
Tokyo

PREFACE

The series *INQUIRY INTO CRUCIAL AMERICAN PROB-LEMS* focuses upon a number of important contemporary social and political issues. Each book presents an in-depth study of a particular problem, selected because of its pressing intrusion into the minds and consciences of most Americans today. A major concern has been the desire to make the materials relevant to students. Every title in the series, therefore, has been selected because, in one way or another, it suggests a problem of concern to students today.

A number of divergent viewpoints, from a wide variety of different *kinds* of sources, encourage discussion and reflection and illustrate that the same problem may be viewed from many different vantage points. Of concern throughout is a desire to help students realize that honest men may legitimately differ in their views.

After a short chapter introducing the questions with which the book will deal, Chapter 2 presents a brief historical and contemporary background so that students will have more than just a superficial understanding of the problem under study. In the readings that follow, a conscientious effort has been made to avoid endorsing any one viewpoint as the "right" viewpoint, or to evaluate the arguments of particular individuals. No conclusions are drawn. Instead, a number of questions for discussion and reflection are posed at the end of each reading so that students can come to their own conclusions.

Great care has been taken to insure that the readings included in each book are just that—readable! We have searched particularly for articles that are of high interest, yet from which differing viewpoints may be legitimately inferred. Whenever possible, dialogues involving or descriptions showing actual people responding and reacting to problematic situations are presented. In sum, each book

- presents divergent, conflicting views on the problem under consideration;

- gives as many perspectives and dimensions on the problem as space permits;

- presents articles on a variety of reading levels, in order to appeal to students of many different ability levels;

- presents analytical as well as descriptive statements;

- deals with real people involved in situations of concern to them;

- includes questions which encourage discussion and thought of the various viewpoints expressed;

- includes activities to involve students to consider further the issues embedded in the problem.

CONTENTS

1

Introduction

Why write a book about prejudice? We all know that prejudice exists, and some of us know a definition: unfounded, overgeneralized, stereotyped thinking formed without a solid assessment of the facts. But knowing a definition doesn't mean much. The chances are that knowledge alone would not prevent one person from calling another human being "nigger," "whitey," "mackerel snapper," or "kike."

There is a simple definition for discrimination, too: prejudice transformed into action. We *think* of a group of people in a certain way (stereotyped thinking) and then promote practices or conditions to support and reinforce our thinking. For example, you are probably familiar with the stereotype of the American Indian as being both incapable and unwilling to adapt to 20th Century America. We see it on TV every time we tune in a Western. This thinking, then, leads to accepting Indian poverty as inevitable. It leads to apathy about reform of reservations; it leads to non-hiring of Indians; and it leads ultimately to the dehumanization of both Indian and white man.

It is important in considering prejudice and discrimination to remember that each represents learned behavior. A learning experience that contributes to prejudice and discrimination may be one in which individuals function as rational, aware human beings. In such instances, there is a conscious effort on the part of the individual to use the learned information in forming a conclusion.

Not all learning experiences, however, are at the conscious level. Many times an individual is not even aware that he is learning a prejudice. The psychologist Harry Stack Sullivan provided some of the clearest explanations of how this could occur. He described how children's attempts to "dramatize" their parent's behavior can lead to similar behavior in the children themselves. The following case study illustrates this point:

1

John was 13 years old when his parents moved from Topeka, Kansas, to a small suburb outside of San Francisco. After three weeks in school he severely beat up a hippie-type fellow student. In John's own words, "I don't dislike hippies. Before we moved Mom and Dad were really upset because we had to move out here around all these long hairs, but it didn't bother me. I don't know why I hit 'em." [1]

John's unconscious prejudice against hippies could have been directed against Blacks or Jews. Could it have been directed against Chevrolets, office managers, or political parties?

Since the Kerner Report [2] brought the subject into the open, examples of unconscious prejudice in our society are constantly being brought to the attention of the public. In their book *Black Rage,* two black psychiatrists "tell it like it is":

The hatred of Blacks has been so deeply bound up with being an American that it has been one of the first things new Americans learn and one of the last things old Americans forget. Such feelings have been elevated to a position of national character, so that individuals now no longer feel personal guilt or responsibility for the oppression of black people. The nation has incorporated this oppression into itself in the form of folkways and storied traditions, leaving the individual free to shrug his shoulders and say only: "That's our way of life." [3]

If the above is true, unconscious acts of prejudice or discrimination may be more significant in our society than conscious actions.

At this point in history prejudice and discrimination appear to be as destructive to human dignity as cannibalism, slavery, and torture were in the past. We like to think of cannibalism, slavery, and torture as learned behavior that is no longer acceptable in civilized society. Participating in such behavior dehumanizes man and strips him of his individualism.

What, then, of prejudice and discrimination? Can we afford to accept the emotional and physical by-products that they produce—humiliation, anger, fear, hate, the ghetto, violence, riots? How much loss of dignity can a man accept? How long can a person submerge his individualism? We have eliminated cannibalism, slavery, and torture; can we now eliminate prejudice and discrimination?

The learning process that produces prejudice and discrimination is

---

[1] Fred Holmes, "John and the Hippie," a case study.
[2] Also known as *The Report of The National Advisory Commission on Civil Disorders,* published in 1968 by the U. S. Government Printing Office.
[3] Excerpted from William H. Grier and Price M. Cobbs, *Black Rage.* New York, N. Y.: Basic Books, Inc., 1968.

a circular one: attitudes are passed from society to the individual and then back from the individual to society. Many examples of this process exist, from the planned violence of sub-groups such as street gang rumbles to more pervading, widespread behavior such as the discrimination against Negroes that exists throughout American society.

The following excerpt from the musical comedy *West Side Story* illustrates this circular learning process. Two street gangs, the Jets and Sharks, meet to arrange a rumble. The Sharks—Bernardo, Chino, Pepe, and Indio—are Puerto Rican Americans whose families moved into New York City in the post-World War II period. The Jets are second- and third-generation Americans whose parents originally came from Europe.

West Side Story, Act II, Scene 6 *

Action:　We got important business comin'.

Doc:　Makin' trouble for the Puerto Ricans?

Snowboy:　They make trouble for us.

Doc:　Look! He almost laughs when he says it. For you, trouble is a relief.

Riff:　We've got to stand up to the PR's, Doc. It's important.

Doc:　Fighting over a little piece of the street is so important?

Action:　To us, it is.

Doc:　To hoodlums, it is. (He goes out through the cellar doorway as Action lunges for him.)

Action:　Don't you call me hoodlum!

Riff:　(Holding him) Easy, Action! Save your steam for the rumble. . . .

Bernardo, Chino, Pepe, and *Indio* enter. [*Doc* has returned.]

Bernardo:　Let's get down to business.

Riff:　Bernardo hasn't learned the procedures of gracious livin'.

Bernardo:　I don't like you, either. So cut it.

Riff:　Kick it, Doc.

Doc:　Boys, couldn't you maybe all talk it—

Riff:　Kick it! (*Doc* goes out. The two gangs take places behind their leaders.)

Riff:　We challenge you to a rumble. All out, once and for all. Accept?

Bernardo:　On what terms?

Riff:　Whatever terms you're callin', buddy boy. You crossed the line once too often.

Bernardo:　You started it.

Riff:　Who jumped A-rab this afternoon?

Bernardo:　Who jumped me the first day I moved here?

---

* Excerpted from Arthur Laurents, Stephen Sondheim, and Leonard Bernstein, *West Side Story*. New York, N. Y.: Random House, 1957.

Action: Who asked you to move here?
Pepe: Who asked you?
Snowboy: Move where you're wanted!
A-rab: Back where ya came from!
Action: Spics!
Pepe: Micks!
Indio: Wop!
Bernardo: We accept!

While street gang society represents one area where prejudice is spawned, many other examples exist. The circular learning process may take place in religious institutions, on Indian reservations, in the female job market, in our homes, or anywhere that individuals meet and trade ideas, fears, and opinions. Prejudice may be conscious or unconscious, hidden or overt, expressed through individual acts or formed into policy by institutions. One thing seems certain: When prejudice develops, political, economic, and social discrimination are rarely very far behind.

How then does one study a topic this complicated? In this book, short articles, both factual and fictional, will be presented to help you form some conclusions about the following questions:

1. Have prejudice and discrimination been widespread in the past?
2. Why do we usually speak of prejudice and discrimination together? Can one exist without the other?
3. Why do men discriminate against their fellows?
4. In what areas of our society do we find discrimination today?
5. How costly are the results of prejudice and discrimination?
6. What solutions might be suggested to the problems of prejudice and discrimination?

Prejudice and Discrimination in the Past

2

Where did it all start? Have you heard of other nations with serious problems of prejudice and discrimination? Is the United States having problems with race for the first time? Have we ever had serious problems with prejudice and discrimination in areas other than race? Has violence always been a part of intolerance?

Anthropologists have evidence that early European nomadic hunters were prejudiced against the more peaceful "fishers and gatherers." This prejudice led to violence and ultimately to the extinction of the "fishers and gatherers."

Far from Europe and at a much later date the Mongols developed a prejudiced view of the Chinese. When they conquered China and established the Yuan Dynasty, their position allowed them to promote discrimination in law, economics, and politics. For example, the law of the land expressly forbade a Chinese from doing bodily harm to a Mongol but made no provision against Mongols doing bodily harm to a Chinese.

In 17th Century Europe prejudice and discrimination were responsible in large part for the colonizing of the New World. Religious persecution of Protestant groups such as the Separatists and Quakers drove many a hardy soul to Plymouth and Pennsylvania. English Courts were closed to Irishmen and Jews, and discriminated against most of those outside court circles in awarding economic monopolies.

While colonies like Maryland and Connecticut were to abolish some of the extreme religious persecution of the Old World, Blue Laws and religious doctrine maintained many discriminatory practices. Puritans in Massachusetts Bay Colony could vote whereas non-Puritans could not;

marriage outside the Church was not acceptable; work on the Sabbath, whether you were a Puritan or not, meant time in the "stocks."

Individuals like Anne Hutchinson and Roger Williams could not accept the prejudice and discrimination of the Massachusetts Bay Colony and spoke out against such practices. Both were banished.

In Maryland Lord Baltimore had hoped to establish a haven for Catholics in the New World. His dream was shattered within twenty years as religious civil war broke out between Catholic and Protestant. The following account is from the Catholic Annual Letter for 1656.

In Maryland, during the years last past, our [Catholic] people have escaped grievous dangers, and have had to contend with great difficulties and straits, and have suffered many unpleasant things, as well from enemies as [from] our own people.

The English who inhabit Virginia had made an attack on the colonists, themselves Englishmen too; and safety being guaranteed on certain conditions, received indeed the governor of Maryland, with many others in surrender. But the conditions being treacherously violated, four of the captives, and three of them Catholics, were pierced with leaden balls. Rushing into our houses, they demanded for death the imposters [i.e., Catholic priests] as they called them, intending inevitable slaughter to those who should be caught. But the Fathers, by the protection of God, unknown to them, were carried from before their faces [i.e., saved]; their books, furniture, and whatever was in the house, fell a prey to the robbers. With almost the entire loss of their property, private and domestic, together with great peril of life, they were secretly carried into Virginia; and in the greatest want of necessaries, scarcely, and with difficulty, do they sustain life. They live in a mean hut low and depressed, not much unlike a cistern, or even a tomb, in which that great defender of the faith, St. Athanasius, lay concealed for many years.[1]

Doctrinal differences between Jew, Catholic, and Protestant led to persecution such as the above. At that time discrimination cut across political, social, and economic lines in both the Old and the New World. Religion influenced voting, trading, and social contacts, particularly during the Colonial Period.

Ethnic prejudice, or prejudice against a particular group of people such as the Dutch or the French, was a serious problem in the colonies and later in the new nation. A belief that the blood of a "pure Englishman" was somehow better than the blood of other men prompted John

---

[1] Excerpted from Thomas A. Baily, ed., *The American Spirit*. Boston, Mass.: D. C. Heath & Co., 1963.

Adams, second President of the United States, to make the following statement:

> New England, in many respects, has the advantage of [over] every other colony in America, and, indeed, of every other part of the world that I know anything of.
> 1. The people are purer English blood; less mixed with Scotch, Irish, Dutch, French, Danish, Swedish, etc., than any other; and descended from Englishmen, too, who left Europe in purer times than the present, and less tainted with corruption than those they left behind them.[2]

The very Constitution established by these Englishmen-turned-Americans discriminated politically against black men by counting them as only ⅗ of a person when figuring representation in Congress. Political discrimination was even greater at the state and local levels, where property, wealth, and family had overwhelming influence.

The Alien and Sedition Acts of 1798 were a striking example of political intolerance. The Federalist Party, fearful that many radical Europeans emigrating to America would engage in treasonable activities (as well as join the rival Republican Party), produced legislation against them. The Alien Act was especially severe. Though passed for a two-year period only, it gave the President of the United States power to eject suspected foreigners from the country by executive order alone.

As for the treatment of Indians, it is a source of shame, through much of our history and to the present day. The following excerpt describes the policy of President Andrew Jackson and some of the early efforts toward "Indian removal."

> Jackson, to the delight of land-hungry Southerners and Westerners, vigorously enforced a plan, favored by both Monroe and Adams and approved by Congress, to remove all the Indian tribes to lands west of the Mississippi. Removal would be better for the Indians themselves, said Jackson, because they were not only unhappy living among the whites but threatened with extinction. "Doubtless it will be painful to leave the graves of their fathers," he conceded, but we need only "open the eyes of those children of the forest to their true condition" to make them appreciate the "humanity and justice" of removal. "Rightly considered," Jackson concluded, "the policy of the General Government toward the red man is not only liberal, but generous."
>
> These unctuous words covered a policy that was callous in its

---

[2] Excerpted from Thomas A. Baily, ed., *The American Spirit*. Boston, Mass.: D. C. Heath & Co., 1963.

conception and often brutal in its execution. Most of the tribes were more or less coerced into signing removal treaties; usually the lands they received in the West were inferior to those they gave up; the migrations themselves were poorly planned and caused much suffering; and in some cases the Indians were literally driven from their old homes by military force. Only a few tribes put up organized re- sistance. In 1832 about a thousand Sac and Fox Indians, led by Chief Black Hawk, defiantly returned to Illinois, but militiamen and army regulars easily drove them back across the Mississippi. This so-called Black Hawk War was hardly more than a skirmish, but the resistance of the Seminoles in Florida was a good deal more for- midable. In 1835 many of them, led by Chief Osceola and supported by scores of runaway slaves, rose in rebellion and thus began a costly war that dragged on into the 1840's. The highly civilized Cherokees of Georgia, on the other hand, tried resistance through legal action. When the government of Georgia refused to recognize their autonomy and threatened to seize their lands, the Cherokees took their case to the Supreme Court and won a favorable decision. Marshall's opinion for the Court majority was that Georgia had no jurisdiction over the Cherokees and no claim to their lands. But Georgia officials simply ignored the decision, and the President refused to enforce it. At length the Cherokees had to leave, too, and when Jackson retired from office he counted the near completion of Indian removals as one of his major achievements.[3]

The Indian was not the only persecuted racial group. Political, economic, and social control of the black man in America has been amply docu- mented. The following excerpt from the autobiography of Frederick Douglass, ex-slave, journalist, and U. S. diplomat, indicates how Southern white men felt about black men in the 1800's.

The frequent hearing of my mistress reading the Bible aloud— for she often read aloud when her husband was absent—awakened my curiosity in respect to this mystery of reading, and roused in me the desire to learn. Up to this time I had known nothing whatever of this wonderful art, and my ignorance and inexperience of what it could do for me, as well as my confidence in my mistress, emboldened me to ask her to teach me to read.

With an unconsciousness and inexperience equal to my own, she readily consented, and in an incredibly short time, by her kind as- sistance, I had mastered the alphabet and could spell words of three or four letters. My mistress seemed almost as proud of my progress as

---

[3] John M. Blum, et al, "Indian Removal," *The National Experience,* 2nd ed. New York, N. Y.: Harcourt, Brace & World, 1968.

if I had been her own child, and supposing that her husband would be as well pleased, she made no secret of what she was doing for me. Indeed, she exultingly told him of the aptness of her pupil, and of her intention to persevere in teaching me, as she felt her duty to do, at least to read the Bible. . . .

Master Hugh was astounded beyond measure, and probably for the first time proceeded to unfold to his wife the true philosophy of the slave system, and the peculiar rules necessary in the nature of the case to be observed in the management of human chattels. Of course, he forbade her to give me any further instruction, telling her in the first place that to do so was unlawful, as it was also unsafe. "For," said he, "if you give a nigger an inch, he will take an ell. Learning will spoil the best nigger in the world. If he learns to read the Bible, it will forever unfit him to be a slave. He should know nothing but the will of his master, and learn to obey it. As to himself, learning will do him no good, but a great deal of harm, making him disconsolate and unhappy. If you teach him how to read, he'll want to know how to write, and this accomplished, he'll be running away with himself." [4]

How could learned Southern gentlemen educated in the supposedly enlightened halls of Northern and European universities accept a practice that absolutely dehumanized a fellow man? There are a number of answers to this question. One could romanticize the whole slave-master relationship and develop a beautiful picture of master and slave living in a Utopia. One might admit that there were problems but argue that these problems were not serious enough to warrant destruction of the Southern economy. One might attempt an "anthropological" explanation, insisting that slaves were mentally inferior. Some Southerners used all these rationalizations and others. Probably the most sweeping defense of slavery employed the use of religion. Jesus Christ and God were invoked to show that the black man had forfeited his right to dignity and worth as a human being. Thornton Stringfellow in *A Scriptural View of Slavery* approached the task in this fashion:

I propose . . . to examine the sacred volume briefly, and if I am not greatly mistaken, I shall be able to make it appear that the institution of slavery has received, in the first place,
1st.   The sanction of the Almighty in the Patriarchal age.
2d.   That it was incorporated into the only National Constitution which ever emanated from God.

---

[4] Excerpted from Thomas A. Baily, ed., *The American Spirit*. Boston, Mass.: D. C. Heath & Co., 1963.

3d. That its legality was recognized, and its relative duties regulated, by Jesus Christ in his kingdom . . .

The first recorded language which was ever uttered in relation to slavery is the inspired language of Noah. In God's stead he says, "Cursed be Canaan"; "a servant of servants shall he be to his brethren." "Blessed be the Lord God of Shem; and Canaan shall be his servant." "God shall enlarge Japheth, and he shall dwell in the tents of Shem; and Canaan shall be his servant."—Gen. ix: 25, 26, 27. Here, language is used, showing the *favor* which God would exercise to the posterity of Shem and Japheth, while they were holding the posterity of Ham in a state of *abject bondage*. May it not be said in truth, that God decreed this institution before it existed; and has he not connected its *existence* with prophetic tokens of special favor, to those who should be slave owners or masters? . . . The sacred records occupy but a short space from this inspired ray on this subject, until they bring to our notice, a man that is held up as a model, in all that adorns human nature, and as one that God delighted to honor. This man is Abraham, honored in the sacred records, with the appellation, "Father" of the "faithful." Abraham was a native of Ur, of the Chaldees. From thence the Lord called him to go to a country which he would show him; and he obeyed, not knowing whither he went. He stopped for a time at Haran, where his father died. From thence he "took Sarai his wife, and Lot his brother's son, and all their substance that they had gathered, and the souls they had gotten in Haran, and they went forth to go into the land of Canaan."—Gen. xii:5.

All the ancient Jewish writers of note, and Christian commentators agree, that by the "souls they had gotten in Haran," as our translators render it, are meant their slaves, or those persons they had bought with their money in Haran. In a few years after their arrival in Canaan, Lot with all he had was taken captive. So soon as Abraham heard it, he armed three hundred and eighteen slaves that were born in his house, and retook him. How great must have been the entire slave family, to produce at this period of Abraham's life, such a number of young slaves able to bear arms.—Gen. xiv:14. . . .

"Thy bond-men and thy bond-maids which thou shalt have, shall be of the heathen that are round about you; of them shall ye buy bond-men and bond-maids. Moreover, of the children of the strangers that do sojourn among you, of them shall ye buy, and of their families that are with you, which they begat in your land. And they shall be your possession. And ye shall take them as an inheritance for your children after you, to inherit them for a possession they shall be your bond-men forever." I ask any candid man, if the words of this institution could be more explicit? It is from God himself; it authorizes that people, to whom he had become *king and law-giver,* to purchase men and women as property; to hold them and their posterity in bondage; and to will them to their children as a possession forever; and more; it allows *foreign slaveholders* to *settle* and *live among them;* to *breed slaves* and *sell them.*[5]

Throughout the 19th Century religious prejudice was stoutly maintained. Political groups such as the Know Nothings, who were anti-Catholic, and the Populists, who were anti-Semitic, flourished. To those groups the whole problem with America was a very simple one—a world conspiracy of Popery, or Jewry, as the case might be, was destroying the fiber and fabric of the country. Every Catholic and every Jew was party to this conspiracy. Discrimination was the natural outcome of such thinking.

Of course, social discrimination also flourished. Marriage between Catholic and Protestant was not sanctioned by the churches concerned without extensive conversion procedures. Private clubs restricted membership on ethnic and religious grounds. In politics, however, changes were noticeable in the eastern United States. The increasing numbers of Irish, Germans, and Italians in the late 1800's were beginning to make their vote significant. Irish and Germans were winning local elections as the 1900's approached.

While the Populists were struggling to save the country from outside elements, the United States was going through an industrial revolution. Ethnic groups from the south of Europe and racial groups from Asia arrived in large numbers to act as labor for an expanding, vital industry. Violence and bloodshed developed as the captains of industry attempted to maintain absolute control over this labor force.

The working class of the 1800's and early 1900's was in large measure composed of immigrants who were treated much as Mexican-Americans, Puerto Ricans, and Blacks are treated today. Composed of Irish, Polish, Italian, and other ethnic minorities, the working class could only complain if factory owners closed their plants with no warning or deprived large numbers of their livelihood. Heavy industry lacked safety rules, and thousands died each year in industrial accidents. Industry used its human labor, including women and children, as a natural resource, without regard for the dignity and worth of the individual. Long regarded as inferior to men, women, especially, were exploited, as the following excerpt illustrates:

---

[5] Excerpted from Eric L. McKitrick, ed., *Slavery Defended: the Views of the Old South.* Englewood Cliffs, N. J.: Prentice-Hall, Inc., 1963.

In Lowell live between seven and eight thousand young women, who are generally daughters of farmers of the different States of New England; some of them are members of families that were rich the generation before . . .

The operatives work thirteen hours a day in the summer time, and from daylight to dark in the winter. At half past four in the morning the factory bell rings, and at five the girls must be in the mills. A clerk, placed as a watch, observes those who are a few minutes behind the time, and effectual means are taken to stimulate to punctuality. This is the morning commencement of the industrial discipline—(should we not rather say industrial tyranny?) which is established in these Associations of this moral and Christian community. At seven the girls are allowed thirty minutes for breakfast, and at noon thirty minutes more for dinner, except during the first quarter of the year, when the time is extended to forty-five minutes. But within this time they must hurry to their boarding-houses and return to the factory, and that through the hot sun, or the rain and cold. A meal eaten under such circumstances must be quite unfavorable to digestion and health, as any medical man will inform us. At seven o'clock in the evening the factory bell sounds the close of the day's work.

Thus thirteen hours per day of close attention and monotonous labor are exacted from the young women in these manufactories. . . .

*   *   *   *   *

Now let us examine the nature of the labor itself, and the conditions under which it is performed. Enter with us into the large rooms, when the looms are at work. The largest that we saw is in the Amoskeag Mills at Manchester. It is four hundred feet long, and about seventy broad; there are five hundred looms, and twenty-one thousand spindles in it. The din and clatter of these five hundred looms under full operation struck us on first entering as something frightful and infernal, for it seemed such an atrocious violation of one of the faculties of the human soul, the sense of hearing. The atmosphere of such a room cannot of course be pure; on the contrary it is charged with cotton filaments and dust, which, we were told, are very injurious to the lungs.

The young women sleep upon an average six in a room, three beds to a room. There is no privacy, no retirement here; it is almost impossible to read or write alone, as the parlor is full and so many sleep in the same chamber. A young woman remarked to us, that if she had a letter to write, she did it on the head of a band-box, sitting on a trunk, as there was not space for a table. So live and toil

the young women of our country in the boarding-houses and manufactories, which the rich . . . have built for them.[6]

Women were forced to struggle for equal rights. The patriarchal, or male-
centered, society of Europe and early America had developed very specific
ideas about womens' place in the world. Women were creatures of the
home; they were to perform the duties of housekeeper, mother, and
obedient wife. At times unmarried women would have to work, but
such a condition was to be avoided at all costs. Recognizing the general
inferiority or desperate need of the job-hunting female, factory and office
managers started the practice very early of paying women less than men.
In addition to suffering from economic inequality, women were denied
political rights until 1920, when they gained the vote. But this did not
greatly change their economic or political position in society.

Labor unions attempted to gain rights for the working man and
woman in much the same fashion as civil rights groups of today are
attempting to gain rights for the black man. The Knights of Labor, in
much the same manner as the NAACP and CORE, wished to end
economic injustice through peaceful, legal, and political means. Early
attempts failed, and action in the form of strikes and violence followed.
The broad masses organized under the A. F. of L. and the C. I. O. used
the strike in much the same spirit as the nonviolent demonstration was
used by CORE and SNCC in the 1950's and early 1960's. However,
peaceful strikes often turned into riots with resulting loss of life and
destruction of property. The violence and destruction in coal and steel
strikes from the late 1800's until the 1940's helped create anti-union
prejudice throughout the land.

Both movements have also had their radical elements. In the labor
movement the International Workers of the World emphasized action
of a violent nature, just as the Black Panthers are doing in the civil
rights struggle of today.

However, the bitterness labor felt for the captains of industry never
did equal the deep-seated hate the slave developed for his white master.
The institution of slavery was unique in its dehumanization of man. Nat
Turner, Denmark Vesey, and other Negro insurrectionists did what most
slaves at one time or another must have yearned to do: to rise up and
smash the white overlord. The Negro rebels were caught and executed,
but for two million other slaves an animal-like existence continued. Even
when he was no longer a slave, the black man was treated in a manner
that seemed to express the judgment of the Constitution years earlier:
his "worth" was about ⅗ of that of a white man. Black Codes herded

---

[6] Excerpted from Raymond S. Iman and Thomas W. Knock, *Labor in American
Society*. Palo Alto, Calif.: Scott, Foresman and Co., 1963.

him into cattle cars and the back of the bus, kept him from voting, deprived him of an education, segregated him in ghettos, and produced an economic system that made advancement practically impossible. Little changed until 1954 when the Supreme Court in *Brown v. Board of Education of Topeka, Kansas,* rendered a decision that struck at segregation and, in effect, freed the black man for the second time. Note the emphasis upon "intangibles" and psychology in the portions of that decision printed below.

We come then to the question presented: Does segregation of children in public schools solely on the basis of race, even though the physical facilities and other "tangible" factors may be equal, deprive the children of the minority group of equal educational opportunities? We believe that it does.

In *Sweatt v. Painter, supra,* in finding that a segregated law school for Negroes could not provide them equal educational opportunities, the Court relied in large part on "those qualities which are incapable of objective measurement but which make for greatness in a law school." In *McLaurin v. Oklahoma State Regents, supra,* the Court, in requiring that a Negro admitted to a white graduate school be treated like all other students, again resorted to intangible considerations: ". . . his ability to study, to engage in discussions and exchange views with other students, and, in general, to learn his profession." Such considerations apply with added force to children in grade and high schools. To separate them from others of similar age and qualifications solely because of their race generates a feeling of inferiority as to their status in the community that may affect their hearts and minds in a way unlikely ever to be undone. The effect of this separation on their educational opportunities was well stated by a finding in the Kansas case by a court which nevertheless felt compelled to rule against the Negro plaintiffs:

> Segregation of white and colored children in public schools has a detrimental effect upon the colored children. The impact is greater when it has the sanction of the law; for the policy of separating the races is usually interpreted as denoting the inferiority of the Negro group. A sense of inferiority affects the motivation of a child to learn. Segregation with the sanction of law, therefore, has a tendency to retard the educational and mental development of Negro children and to deprive them of some of the benefits they would receive in a racially integrated school system.

Whatever may have been the extent of psychological knowledge at the time of *Plessy v. Ferguson,* this finding is amply supported by modern authority. Any language in *Plessy v. Ferguson* contrary to this finding is rejected.

We conclude that in the field of public education the doctrine of "separate but equal" has no place. Separate educational facilities are inherently unequal. Therefore, we hold that the plaintiffs and others similarly situated for whom the actions have been brought are, by reason of the segregation complained of, deprived of the equal protection of the laws guaranteed by the Fourteenth Amendment.[7]

Although the Court was very clear in its decision, the country was less clear in its response. Southern schools remain largely segregated years later. Yet much has happened. The black man is gaining a new self-awareness and a sense of pride in his heritage and accomplishments, made against such heavy odds. He is angry and more and more is applying pressure through violence as well as in the Courts, to force equal economic and political opportunity.

Whites and Blacks are examining and attacking the entire spectrum of prejudice and discrimination—religious, racial, social, economic, and political. Change is slow, but gains are being made: Equal Opportunity employers are more numerous, and such policies are enforced by law. Unions are beginning to open their doors. Professions are opening up. In politics Blacks and Jews have been elected to the Senate, a Catholic and a Quaker have been elected to the Presidency, and Blacks are beginning to take advantage of their voting power. Women are being mentioned as Vice-Presidential candidates and increasingly are demanding—and getting—equal pay for equal work.

Problems of tremendous magnitude remain. The black man is still socially segregated and trapped in the ghetto. American Indians live in squalid conditions, almost totally outside the political and social structure. Economic conditions are poor for Puerto Ricans and Mexican-Americans. Job opportunities for women rarely reach the management level.

Historically, progress has continued, though often only after great pressure. Will we require still more pressure from minorities before we achieve our long-stated goal: a society with liberty and justice for all?

What Do You Think?

1. What factors contributed to the acceptance of the labor movement?

2. What factors would you say contributed to a decrease in prejudice and discrimination on a large scale against Catholics in the United States?

---

[7] Excerpted from *Brown v. Board of Education of Topeka* (347 U. S. 483), unanimous decision of the United States Supreme Court, 1954.

3.   What factors might contribute to a decrease in prejudice and discrimination for black men?

ACTIVITIES FOR INVOLVEMENT

1.   The chances are very good that sometime in the past your family has faced prejudice and discrimination. From your parents find out as much as you can about your family tree. Then, using U. S. History and American literature books, find out what types of social injustice plagued your family. If you are a minority group student, find out when prejudice and discrimination were first felt by your ancestors.

2.   Investigate a particular group's contribution to the culture of the United States (Spanish, Japanese, Negro, Chinese, Jewish, Irish, etc.).

3.   President Jackson moved many Indians west of the Appalachians. Throughout the 1800's, peace treaties and congressional settlements were broken and Indians forced to move. One of the most agonizing of the moves concerned Chief Joseph and the Nez Perce Indians. Research either the story of Chief Joseph, or, try to uncover what happened to the Indians that were settled in your state when it was first occupied by white men.
Why do you feel Indians were moved from reservation to reservation? Were Indians protected by the Constitution? Why or why not?

4.   Using the *Readers' Guide to Periodical Literature,* research government policy toward reservations today. Is change taking place? In light of the Brown vs Topeka, Kansas, Board of Education ruling by the Supreme Court, is such segregation legal? Break into small groups and discuss the question, "Are Indians segregated socially, emotionally, politically, and economically by the reservation system?" Be sure to consider the emotional impact of reservation life upon the individual.

5.   At the request of numerous government officials, President Franklin Delano Roosevelt, in 1942, signed an "executive order" leading to the legal and absolute removal of all Japanese from the Pacific Coast. The major reason cited was that the presence of Japanese-Americans and Japanese nationals on the Pacific Coast constituted a threat to the security of the area specifically and the nation generally. In the colonial period Roger Williams, Anne Hutchinson, and their followers were felt to be a threat to the security of the Massachusetts Bay Colony. Later, the Indians were felt to be a threat to the security of the settlers.
How valid do you feel is this reasoning? Could there be other reasons for forced movements? How did the Supreme Court rule in the case of the Japanese? Using the concept of the threat to the community, is it possible that black citizens might be moved out of the cities if the white population feels they constitute a threat to the security of the white population?

6.   In the 1935 Wagner Act, labor gained a legal right to strike and federal government assurances that collective bargaining would take place between management and labor. As a result of this legislation, working conditions and salaries have improved.

Under present conditions, is the use of the strike still a valid instrument for labor? In the past few years we have seen the strike used on campus to effect change. Is this a valid use of the strike? What about use of the strike by doctors, teachers, police, or firemen? Has your answer to any of the above questions been affected by prejudice? Have you discriminated in your answers? Explain.

3

Prejudice and Discrimination Today

Does a cause-and-effect relationship exist between prejudice and discrimination? Can we say that a person who is prejudiced will discriminate, or that a person who discriminates is prejudiced? Is it possible to be prejudiced and not realize it? May a person see prejudice where it does not exist?

In this chapter you will read articles and incidents demonstrating the nature of prejudice and its relationship to discrimination.

1. MESSAGE OF HATE ON A NEGRO'S HOME *

At times, prejudice is not subtle but appears as sheer hate. What could have promoted this incident? Is this an example of discrimination?

Richard Dixon, an ordinary man who wanted a home for his family, bought a house in the Sunset District two weeks ago. Someone didn't like Richard and Patricia Dixon and their three children having a home there because they are Negroes. Early yesterday morning that someone spelled out his hate.

He (or she or they) got a can of spray paint and, across the green center panel of the Dixons' garage at 4430 Kirkham St., he expressed his venom: "Nigger Go Home." It was signed "KKK" for the Ku Klux Klan.

"I'm not beating an integration drum," said the 30 year old mailman

---

* From the San Francisco *Examiner,* October 25, 1962.

yesterday. "All my wife and I want is a house that's adequate to our family needs."

"It's such a sneaky thing to do. If this person would come and ring my doorbell, maybe I could talk to him. But he's not even giving me a chance this way." . . .

"When we bought the house we didn't do it to prove anything. We don't feel we have to prove we're good Americans. Actions speak louder than words. Whoever did it certainly hasn't taken our actions into consideration. We saved years and years to buy this house."

"The neighbors have been very courteous," said Mrs. Dixon, "and the children haven't had any difficulty. They've been invited into other homes to play." Dixon who, like his wife, is a high school graduate, said that when he returned home from work Tuesday afternoon something illegible had been scrawled on his garage.

"I thought maybe it was just kids," he said. "I wiped it off. But this morning—there was no mistaking it."

Said Mrs. Dixon, petite and gently-spoken: "I feel a little sick and a little frightened."

What Do You Think?

1. Was Richard Dixon's reaction to the "Message of Hate" a normal reaction when prejudice is involved? Explain.

2. Could there be an explanation other than prejudice for the "Message of Hate"?

2. A JUDGE'S DOUBLE STANDARD *

A municipal judge is questioned about decisions of law for which he was responsible. Did the judge base his decision upon a point of law? Would you have ruled in the same fashion?

Municipal Judge Bernard Glickfield ruled yesterday on the case of three well-scrubbed youths who attacked some starlight picnickers near Sigmund Stern Grove (in San Francisco, California) ten days ago.

The judge, famed for his tirades against the slovenly appearance of beatnik types, said the youths were victims of "bad associations and poor judgment."

He gave them six-month suspended jail sentences and 90 days pro-

---

* From the *San Francisco Chronicle*, May 18, 1963.

bation each despite Assistant District Attorney Luther Goodwin's plea that they spend five weekends in jail.

The youths who pleaded guilty to misdemeanor battery charges were between 18 and 20 years of age and were residents of San Francisco.

They were arrested with three 17 year old boys on May 4 after they attacked four University of California students and their girl friends at the grove. . . .

Only last month Judge Glickfield sentenced nine young men in need of hair cuts to five days each in jail for cavorting in Alamo Square at 2 A.M.

Although those youths committed no violence against anyone, Judge Glickfield castigated them in court for "your foolish actions."

"You're the filthiest bunch I've ever seen" he stormed. "You're just filthy. I would hate to think that any of you were related to me." Asked why he gave jail sentences to the Alamo Square group and not to the Sigmund Stern Grove attackers, the judge said: "These boys today were chastened, while the others were not. These kids come from fine families, long-time families in San Francisco. I've talked to their parents."

Judge Glickfield said the Alamo Square group had "no sense of social responsibility, no idea they were doing something wrong."

"And they had all just landed in San Francisco from other parts of the country," he added. "I'm known as a tough judge, and I made my decision in good conscience," the judge concluded.

What Do You Think?

1. Is Judge Glickfield interpreting with his own prejudices or mirroring the views of the courts? How do you know?
2. Does the judge's decision constitute discrimination against long hair and nonconformity?
3. Is the judge's decision justified? If so, on what grounds?

3. PROBLEMS FOR NEGRO VETS *

Black veterans of Vietnam have found their service ribbons and Purple Hearts do not make them exceptions to society's racism. Under such circumstances is it any wonder that some black men are beginning to question black involvement in the armed forces?

Willie Hampton, 23, is a San Franciscan and twice wounded veteran of the Vietnamese conflict. He represents what is considered most de-

---

* From the San Francisco *Examiner,* March 11, 1968.

sirable in American manhood—young, trained, disciplined, and employable, with all service commitments fulfilled. . . .

Willie Hampton also is a Negro. He earns $385 a month working in a local hospital at a job roughly equivalent to that of a vocational nurse.

It is a job in which he can use his service-learned skills, for Hampton was a medical corpsman with the airborne troops. In fact, he has more Army-learned skills than his job requires.

He shares a rundown apartment with a young male friend at 806 Oak Street. He wants his own apartment in a better neighborhood but he also is discovering that serving one's country is no magic door opener to a prejudiced landlord.

"It's rough," Hampton observes. "I went to a lady at Eddy and Divisadero streets who had an apartment to rent. She takes one look at me and says: 'Somebody beat you to it.' " . . .

Still, Hampton believes there are more opportunities in the Bay Area for Negro veterans than in other localities. He bases much of his view on what occurred during his post-combat visit to his family in rural Tunica.

Tunica is near the Tennessee-Mississippi border and just a rifle shot from where Negro civil rights leader James Meredith was gunned down on a Mississippi road. . . .

On Aug. 20, 1966, Hampton hobbled into the Cotton Boll Cafe. He was clad in the suntan khaki uniform he had worn on extended convalescent leave.

On his shoulder, he wore the patch of the 173rd Airborne Division, an organization of great pride and formidable military ability.

His right leg was encased in the cast shielding knee and ankle wounds suffered the preceding January when a claymore mine exploded near the South Vietnamese capitol of Saigon.

Two months earlier, the shoulder covered by the division patch had been shattered by a grenade in War Zone D. But the wound healed enough for Hampton to return to combat. . . .

He recalls he was barely in the front door of the cafe before a waitress looked at him coldly and said: "You can't come in here. You'll have to go to the back."

She indicated a rear door, termed the "colored entrance." There was a small room of spindly chairs and battered tables where black people were served.

Near the front door was a man sprawled in an upholstered chair before a well-appointed table reserved for white patrons. He looked at Hampton and said without particular rancor: "You better get in back, nigger!"

The cafe's white owner—"I used to play football with his son," recalls Hampton—shoved the young soldier and he was out on the street.

It was because of incidents like this, plus a pointed admonishment from Tunica police to leave town as a troublemaker, that Hampton decided to . . . return to San Francisco.

"It's better here," said Hampton. "There is less prejudice. You are called a nigger down there and there is nothing you can do about it. Here, you at least can talk back."

What Do You Think?

1. If you were Willie Hampton from Tunica, Tennessee, how would you react to the kind of treatment he received in the Tunica cafe? Explain.
2. Why do you think discrimination is so open in the South and so covert in the West?

4.   A HIGH SCHOOL SENIOR SPEAKS *

Are the attitudes of high school seniors the same throughout the United States? Compare your responses to those of this young man living in a small farming community eighty miles south of San Francisco, California.

(Q) Do you have any minority groups in Hollister?

(A) Negroes? No, we don't have any of those.

(Q) How about farm workers?

(A) Oh yeah, but they don't live here all year round. Oh, if you mean Mex Wetbacks we got some of them. Some Mex families live here all year.

(Q) What kind of work do they do?

(A) Stoop labor—that's man killin' if you never done it—picking beans or artichokes or berries. Some pick fruit. Some work on the [hay] bailers, but they're not too good. Too lazy.

(Q) Too lazy?

(A) Yeah, can't stay workin' in the sun like a white kid.

(Q) Why not?

(A) I dunno, probably not as well fed, probably not in as good shape. Maybe they're just weaker.

---

* A taped interview made by Fred R. Holmes.

(Q) Could they be?

(A) Yeah, I guess, they're always a lot smaller too. Probably why they always want to use a knife when they fight. Buddy of mine was caught by three of the Wetbacks and really cut up—no reason either. They're like that—cut you up for no reason at all!

(Q) How do they do in school?

(A) Not much—The Wets don't go, and the ones that live here are kinda dumb.

(Q) Why do you think the Wets skip school?

(A) Why ask me! They probably don't like it.

(Q) What about the houses they live in?

(A) Man, are those shacks filthy—even the ones that live here. They could at least get some whitewash and tarpaper. They're really not too good at saving, except what they send home to Mexico.

(Q) Do you know any of these Mex kids?

(A) No man—you know that white kids don't hang around with Mex's.

(Q) Why not?

(A) They don't eat or drink like us, we like different music, and they can't talk worth a hoot 'n a holler. Tough to get on with them— they won't let any of their women go out with "the guys." I'm sure I don't have to take their guff. We've got them just where we want them! They're dirty too.

(Q) What do you mean, "just where we want them?"

(A) You know, as long as they stay in their place it's O. K., I like them fine. But not in the drugstore or where we play pool. They could be as good as us, I guess. Maybe they don't have the brains or the build. That's probably it.

(Q) Any prejudice out here in the country?

(A) Oh, yeah, some guys really hate the Niggers, er, Negroes, nothin' else.

(Q) What about discrimination?

(A) Naw—these guys can go anywhere they want to. They hardly ever come to the same hangouts; they've got their own. Nothin' ever happens when one goes to the drive-in for hamburgers. I don't know about Negroes, if they came.

(Q) Would there be a difference?

(A) I dunno, maybe—well, I just don't know.

What Do You Think?

1. How would you explain this teen-ager's responses?
2. The speaker remarked that he didn't know any "Mex" kids. Where do you suppose, then, that he got all his information? How valid do you think such information is?
3. Can the speaker's views be changed? How?

5. THE BITTERNESS *

It is too easy, in looking at racial problems, to assume that all will be solved by providing equal opportunity, equal housing, and equal schooling. In the long run this may be so, but it sometimes ignores the resentment that has accumulated in the individual from past slights, his super-sensitive feelings, his anger. Mr. August is a black student from South Africa, now living in London; could his feelings and experiences be those of a black American as well?

"Lamb cutlets? . . . There . . . Mash or chips? . . . Peas? . . . Gravy for you?" . . .

Now you had finished serving me and were handing over the plate and with the smile still in your voice you said, "There you are, my boy."

But I dislike any white person calling me "boy." First, I am circumcised and, therefore, not a boy. Second, I am tired of hearing a gardener called a garden-boy, a policeman police-boy, a postman post-boy, and so on, just because they are black.

But you said it so naturally that I hardly noticed it and so did not remember to feel insulted. Usually I feel insulted, especially when my white "friends" say it with their studied camaraderie. But not with you, dear lady. I did not even notice it until, unfortunately, you made me—by becoming very embarrassed. You put your hand to your mouth and said in a very apologetic voice, "Oh, dear, dear! What have I said now? Please forgive me, sir."

How could I forgive when I had not felt offended? But I couldn't stand there and explain—Mr. Lyons would not have liked it if I had slowed down his business. I hope, dear lady, you see this, because I'm writing it for you. You are the kind of Yahoo who, just as I am about to curse your fellow Yahoos, helps preserve my not-so-stable sanity.

Dear lady, most of your race are rotten—unfortunately for me,

---

* Excerpted from "The Bitterness," by Collingwood August. Reprinted from *Atlas Magazine*, June 1965, from *Spectator*, London.

because they make me as rotten as they are. Let me tell you a few stories to show what I mean.

When first I came here I went for an interview for a job with a county council—no names, please. The three wise monkeys who perceive no evil were sitting cosily round their table. I came in from the English winter into this stuffy, smelly room. We went through the preliminary mumbo-jumbo fairly easily and I was beginning to think that I had the job in my pocket.

"Tell us," the stiff collar in the middle brayed in his ruling class voice, "in your form you state that you were, for some years, a school-teacher. Why did you stop teaching?"

"I resigned."

"Why?"

"I disagreed with my government's education policy."

"Why did you disagree?" the running nose on the right asked.

"It's against my conscience to teach black children that they are inferior to white children."

"So you disagree with your employers and, when you do, you just leave them like that?" the thin dry gorilla lips on the left snapped his fingers.

"What else is there to do?" I foolishly countered.

At this stage the chairman of the Star Chamber changed the subject. "Now, this newspaper you say you were editor of—what kind of man owned it?" You ugly-minded buzzard, I thought to myself, let's have a few games while we may. So I deliberately misunderstood the question.

"A very good man," I answered.

"No, I'm afraid you've misunderstood me. What I mean was, er . . . (out with it, say it for yourself, I shan't help you—you Godforsaken fascist) er . . . was he a white or colored gentleman?"

"Is that relevant?"

"Oh yes, it is. We like to know these things."

"Gentlemen, thank you for the interview." I stood up. "But just for your information, his father was a governor-general and a 'sir'." I closed the door gently behind me—for England had already taught me that gentlemen never lose their tempers. I hated the bastards. . . .

*   *   *   *   *

One thing I'll never understand about your people, dear lady, is why they expect us to be better people than they are: we must return their evil with good . . .

In a pub where I'm not a regular the regulars decided to bring me into their drinking school. After a lot of conversation, one of them remarked: "It's a pleasure to meet an educated colored gentleman like you. I didn't know there were any." His friends nodded their acquiescence.

I returned the compliment with, "It's a pleasure to meet uneducated white people like you. I didn't know there were any." The barman threw me out.

What Do You Think?

1. How do you think Mr. August felt when his acquaintance referred to him as "an educated colored gentleman"? Explain.
2. Was Mr. August upset primarily over prejudiced thinking directed toward him or discriminatory action directed against him? Explain.
3. Could the waitress or "the three wise monkeys" be accused of prejudiced thought or discriminating action? Explain.

6.   DISCRIMINATION? YES, BUT IT'S DIRECTED AT WOMEN *

Too often we think of prejudice and discrimination only as they apply to minority groups. Women have struggled for equality in the past; have they achieved their goal?

Want ads discriminate against women, says Assistant Secretary of Labor, Esther Peterson.

Listing jobs under "male" and "female" labels is a barrier, she says, and "it is women's work that is underpriced and underpaid. Many of our assumptions about 'male' and 'female' jobs are false. Job labeling comes about through an unquestioning acceptance of certain assumptions about femininity and masculinity. It's self-deception, and we're all guilty of it."

Writing for a Department of Labor pamphlet, Mrs. Peterson lists four assumptions under which "male" and "female" jobs are listed. She says they are all wrong.

1.   *Woman's place is in the home.*

Mrs. Peterson says: "Of course it is! And so is the man's and the children's. The home is the main place for all of us. Just yesterday, woman's only work place was in the home, a full-time job.

"Today, though, much of her former work is being done for her, through mass production and modern packaging and processing. Inside-the-home jobs have shrunk. She has the time, the energy and the spirit to work."

2.   *Women don't have to—and therefore shouldn't—work.*

Mrs. Peterson says: "Another version of this goes, 'Women work

---

* From the *Oakland Tribune,* January 14, 1968.

only for pin money.' We must remember that the pin money may mean hairpins for some, but for others it means diaper pins and hard-earned essentials. For most working wives, the 'luxuries' they afford means college educations for their children and paying doctor bills."

3. *Mothers should be with their young children.*

Mrs. Peterson says: "Of course they should! As much as they can be and want to be. Almost every woman I know agrees with this. But what of those many, many working mothers who are widowed, divorced, or separated? What of the women whose husband's paychecks can't be stretched to meet the family needs?

"Moralizing about this is simply demoralizing to mothers who have to, or who want to, work."

4. *People just don't like women bosses.*

Mrs. Peterson says: "This one, I think, we're going to find simply evaporating in the light of experience, as more and more people work with and for, women."

There's been a great movement of women—into the labor force since World War II.

In 1940, women made up one fourth of the labor force. Today there are 28.7 million working women, more than one-third of all jobs in the country.

Today, almost half of the women of working age—those 18 to 64—are working. Three out of five women holding jobs are married.

Mrs. Peterson says the only question an employer should ask of a woman is the same he should ask of a man: "Is she willing and able?"

What Do You Think?

1. Do the four "assumptions" listed by Esther Peterson constitute prejudice? Why or why not?
2. Do you think of certain jobs as "male" and others as "female"? Explain.
3. Is the only question an employer should ask of a woman "Is she willing and able"?

7. RACE PREJUDICE BY WHITE CHRISTIANS *

Sociologists have discovered some remarkable conditions relating to prejudice, as the following article illustrates. Can discovery or awareness alter prejudiced thought?

---

* "Race Prejudice by White Christians," by Donovan Bess, *San Francisco Chronicle,* March 26, 1968.

A University of California sociologist reported yesterday that prejudice against Negroes flourishes among America's white Christians, especially among active church members.

And a UC research psychologist reported that such racial prejudice also is rampant among teen-age school children. He said their teachers are doing almost nothing about it.

The social scientists presented their findings on the Berkeley campus before 300 participants in a symposium on prejudice.

The sociologist, Rodney Stark, said nationwide research on white Christian attitudes brought him to conclude: "On Sunday morning those Americans who most need to have their prejudice shaken are more likely to be found in church than home reading the newspapers or watching the football game of the week."

Stark, reporting on conclusions reached with Charles Y. Glock, chairman of the sociology department at Berkeley, said the majority of white American church members "hold religious and racial prejudice and they deny the right of the churches to challenge their prejudices."

Investigators have found, he said, that between half and two-thirds of the country's Christians "would deny civil liberties to a person who does not believe in God" and "would bar him from holding public office and remove him from a teaching position in the public schools."

FAITH

He reported that the majority of Christian laymen "may claim to love their brothers, but they are very finicky about whom they call 'brother'."

Stark said the UC investigations sought to find out how far the practicing Christian carries out the ethical credo of his faith as summed up in advice such as "Love thy neighbor" and "Do good unto others."

The sociologists said that, "while the ethics taught by the church are a potent weapon against prejudice, it is not at all clear that the churches can claim a direct credit for this fact.

"Instead, we found that those church members who have accepted the other doctrines of the church or who regularly attend the church or participated in church activities were somewhat less likely to accept Christian ethicalism."

He and Glock concluded that before the churches "can truly aid the cause of brotherhood they will have to decide more clearly what it is they want their members to believe."

Some astringent comments on these findings were made by Noel D. Freedman, an Old Testament scholar and on the faculty of the San Francisco Theological Seminary.

Freedman said these prejudiced Christians were in a theological sense "faithful to the history of the church" since the theme of inequality permeates the Bible.

TESTAMENT

"If the followers of Christianity cling to their prejudices, it is because they feel it is an essential part of their religion." He said, "the New Testament is simply an anti-Semitic book."

The Bible scholar recalled that only a century ago the issue of slavery had been ardently debated in American religious circles.

"Every figure in the Old Testament has slaves," he said. "The Israelites who went out of Egypt took their slaves with them. Here is this great crusade for freedom!"

What Do You Think?

1. Does this article shed any light upon who determines whether the individual will think in a prejudiced fashion?
2. What does the sociologist mean when he says that the majority of white American church members "hold religious and racial prejudice and they deny the right of the churches to challenge their prejudices?" Would you agree? Explain.

8.   A LAST STAND IN OAKLAND *

What effect would constant discrimination have upon you? Stella Leach has faced that problem.

A native American family, more American than the descendants of the Mayflower, has decided to make a last stand against what they call vicious discrimination in a sedate Bay Area neighborhood. "I'm tired of moving at least once a year because people don't seem to like the fact that we're Indians," said Stella Leach, divorced mother of six and a proud, graceful member of the Ogallala Sioux nation. "This time we're going to stand by our guns."

Mrs. Leach, a nurse for Dr. David Tepper and volunteer head of the American-Indian Well Baby Clinic, said her Oakland home at 3112 Kingsland Street—in the shadow of Mills College—has been "under siege and harassment" since she moved there in February.

Mrs. Leach said she first rented the modest two-bedroom home—at $150 a month—through Al Marcotte, Hayward realtor, acting for Gladys Parenti of San Leandro, owner of the house.

"All they asked me," Mrs. Leach recalled, "was if I was Italian. All I said was 'no'."

---

* "A Last Stand in Oakland," by Michael Grieg, *San Francisco Chronicle*, May 25, 1968.

Then, she said, the neighbors found out she and her six children—one of them, Harry, a Silver Star hero in Vietnam—were Indian. At first, they just didn't speak to us. Then the phone calls started—obscene calls. Complaints to the police, she said, were useless. Or worse—"the police would tell us we were in the wrong, and the kids were making too much noise." . . .

As for Mrs. Leach, she remained stubbornly proud of being a red American. "One of our fine neighbors told a son of mine that he 'certainly had a strange mother,'" she said. "Sure, I like to put on dungarees and wear moccasins around the house. Yes, and I like to let my hair down and invite the kids of the neighborhood over and show them how we dance.

"What do they want me to do—bleach my face, cut my hair, and look like a white woman? Frankly, I never found that much nice about white women."

Then on Wednesday, Mrs. Leach said, the harassment increased. "We came home and found the front door gone. The house was in a shambles. There were broken dishes all around. And Mike's war bonnet—a gift from his grandfather—had all the precious eagle feathers pulled out. Why, they even ripped out his hi-fi set and stole a camera and typewriter." . . .

On top of all that, she said, there was a letter from the realtor announcing that the $150 rent had been boosted to $400. "They really want us out," she said dryly.

What Do You Think?

1. Under such pressure, how long would an individual be able to maintain and demonstrate Indian traditions?
2. Under such conditions should one attempt to maintain cultural traditions? Explain.

9. WHAT'S NOT SO FUNNY ABOUT THE FUNNIES *

Few black people appear in the comic strips. Have you ever wondered why?

What would happen if Mr. & Mrs. America turned to the comics one Sunday morning and found a Negro detective working with Dick Tracy,

---

* Excerpted from "What's Not So Funny About the Funnies," *Ebony*, November 1966.

a Negro intern on the staff of Rex Morgan or some Negroes living next door to Blondie? The shock could be fatal. On the other hand, it could be the best thing that ever happened in comicdom.

Negroes, of course, are not alien to the strips. For years Joe Palooka had a trusty valet named Smokey ("a shuffling, servile caricature who spoke perfect stereotype") and Joe could hardly move around the race track without Asbestos. Mush-mouth characters also walked in and out of old-timers like Happy Hooligan, Barney Google, and, as late as the 50's, Moon Mullins. No matter where they appeared, however, they all shared one trait: unbelievably big lips and solid black skin ovaled into a stupid looking face. They talked the same language, too, which invariably sounded like, "Boss, ah's fwightened 'bout Spahky—he walks lak he wuz lame."

Smokey, Asbestos and their caricatured friends might have aged without ever changing. But in the early '40's, America went through a World War which domestically liberated Negroes from the acceptance (if not the reality) of second-class citizenship. Fighting overseas and working side by side with whites on assembly lines convinced many a Negro he had more to offer than a tradition of laziness, blindly-drawn minstrel features and faithful service.

Once funny, Negroes in the comics became reprehensible. The NAACP told McNaught Syndicate that Smokey was an insult to the American Negro, and Joe Palooka woke up one day minus his valet. Other Negroes wondered why they had to be a porter, maid, or stable boy to make the strips and many more charged that the Negro always came out on the bottom. The storm of protest was so great that the only black characters remaining when it subsided were "natives" like Lothar in Mandrake the Magician, and those found in Tarzan and in the Phantom.

While cartoonists might have thought all the hullabaloo was silly ("Why, Negroes have always been drawn like that"), they could not afford to ignore the indictment. With the demise of Smokey, Negroes—caricatures or otherwise—became noticeably absent from the comic pages.

Any cartoonist who thought that getting rid of the old stereotypes might soothe sensitive souls, soon found out, however, exclusion was not the answer. "They really didn't understand what was bugging us," observes a Negro man. "Instead of rectifying the situation, they just dropped it." Negroes were not asking to be taken out of the strips. They simply wanted the caricatures replaced—or at least balanced by characters with whom they could identify. Domestics, and even soldiers, might have reflected the limited job opportunities once available to Negroes. But changing times had also made room for professionals. Negro lawyers, secretaries, engineers, business executives could be found everywhere, the complaint went, except in the comics.

Few cartoonists can argue. . . .

With gag-a-day strips increasing in popularity, the cartoonists' problems are compounded. Bob Dunn of "They'll Do It Every Time" and "Little Iodine" fame loves to exaggerate his characters, "to give them big schnozzes, big feet, big ears." A Negro character drawn in the same tradition might not win laughs from Negroes. "Let's say I put a colored guy in a bar," says Dunn. "I'm not sure I could let myself go. I'd have to be sure he's sweet and nice and not offensive." Currently president of the National Cartoonists Society, Dunn offers another example: "If I draw a lazy-looking white guy lounging around in his underwear, it's all right. But if that same guy happens to be a Negro, there would be letters. Why? Some people would feel I'm saying all colored people lie around the house in their underwear."

Other cartoonists agree: caricatures are meant to make people look and act funny. Negroes, they maintain, have not reached the point where they can laugh at themselves. Explains Sylvan Byck, King Features Syndicate (KFS) comics editor for the past 20 years: "You have a white lawyer and he turns out to be a crook. No one says anything. But if he is a Negro it's no longer funny." Or as Al Capp, creator of Li'l Abner, puts it: "The day we can draw a Negro girl or boy in caricature or a funny situation, the civil rights movement will be over."

Whatever reasons are offered to explain or excuse the relative absence of Negroes in the comics, they all add up to one thing—economics. There are more than 250 different strips and panels syndicated in some 1,700 daily newspapers and read by more than 100 million Americans virtually any day in the year. A top strip can bring a cartoonist $300 to $3,000 or more a week. In an industry where competition stiffens more each year (out of some 1,000 strips submitted to one syndicate in 12 months, only two to three make it) and dying newspapers continue to shrink the market, most cartoonists, syndicates, and papers are not anxious to do anything that might offend even one reader.

Said one cartoonist: "If an editor gets one letter complaining about something, it carries more weight than 100 good ones. If one cartoon amuses 100,000 people but offends one, the editors make you change it." For the same reasons a syndicate comics editor candidly asks: "Why should I have to ask a guy to worry about every word he says. There is no advantage to a cartoonist to bring Negro characters in a strip, just the horror of controversy. If I were a cartoonist, I wouldn't want to be a crusader, especially if I felt I would lose the strip."

While Negroes—and other ethnic minorities—may be "understandably touchy" about their portrayal in menial or demeaning roles, it is difficult to see why a Negro teacher or other professional might be offensive. He might be a bitter pill for readers unaccustomed to regarding Negroes as anything but servants, answer cartoonists who are not particularly eager to use their "million dollar property" to enlighten them.

An even greater drawback, however, is the bad taste which impassioned letters against Smokey left for many cartoonists. Although there is a difference between a valet (who admittedly could annoy Negroes) and an attorney (who realistically could represent one of the many Negroes practicing law in the country) cartoonists are not ready to "open up the wounds" by using a Negro in any capacity. . . .

Even if an "integrated strip" is drawn by a Negro cartoonist, there is no guarantee of acceptance. Last year, 42-year-old Morrie Turner brought Wee Pals to the comic world. Only nine papers throughout the country have taken it on. The gag-a-day strip focuses on interracial relations. Its cast of caricatured 5 to 12 year olds includes Oliver, white, ("He's a little intellectual," Turner explains. "He sort of knows it all. He's a composite of the many people I've known"); Connie, also white, who is very aggressive ("If she believes something is right, she will punch anyone who disagrees"); and Randy, Negro, who is Oliver's best friend ("He has a passion for words. They fascinate him"). There is also Sybil Wright, a play on civil rights, who is "like all the sweet little Negro girls you ever meet. There's no hatred in her soul at all"; Nipper, who wears a Confederate cap which "shows you how much he knows about race relations"; and George who is very Oriental in spite of his name ("I wanted everyone to be able to identify with him"). . . .

Turner admits he launched his strip with a defeatist attitude. "I was pretty negative I guess. I sent it to the United Features and told them because of its limited appeal they probably wouldn't be interested. They wrote back and said I was absolutely right." Papers which have gambled on Wee Pals, syndicated by Lew Little in San Francisco, include the Oakland Tribune, Philadelphia Bulletin, Detroit News, San Diego Tribune and Los Angeles Times. . . .

When racing expert Ken Kling began drawing Joe and Asbestos back in 1925, there were no complaints even though Asbestos, modeled after famous Negro jockey Isaac Murphy, sported a black face, rubber lips and certain dialect ("Dis platter should win de final trot"). For years Asbestos never changed although the strip was faithfully followed by millions looking for horse tips. Then, about three years ago, Kling heard from CORE. "They thought the lips were too exaggerated. They asked me if I would kindly change the features and make Asbestos more human." Overnight Asbestos became a new man. He had already learned a new vocabulary. Now he was lighter, smaller, and maybe even handsome. "I made him look like a regular person, less grotesque." Kling, who grew up in Harlem, the son of an Alsatian butcher, insists his original caricature was not intended to be malicious. "When we draw cartoons, we make all kinds of silly caricatures. We don't mean any harm. Cartoonists don't want to make people look bad. We do it for fun—to make people laugh." What was his reaction to CORE? "I wasn't mad.

When the strip started, minstrels were popular. I was glad to cooperate in any way I could. I changed him immediately." . . .

Negroes are so conditioned to not seeing themselves in the comics in any favorable light that when they do get in they are apt not to notice it.

Al Capp, one of the most successful cartoonists around, admits: "It makes me so damn mad when someone comes up and complains that Negroes are not in the strips." In one of his Li'l Abner strips, Capp put Sammy Davis Jr. on a board of directors. Although a Negro was in a "situation of eminent authority," not one of Capp's nearly 80 million readers said a word—except Davis himself who wrote the cartoonist saying he had noticed it. He has also used Godfrey Cambridge and Ralph Bunche in the strip.

With the appearance of a Negro in anything but a menial capacity almost unheard of, readers often overlook the fact, too, that Negro soldiers have been in the strips for so long that their presence is now passé. In fact if it hadn't been for a Negro soldier, American hero Steve Canyon might not be alive today.

Years ago when Milton Caniff was doing Terry and the Pirates, he received a letter from a friend who had attended a lecture in Chicago where publishing magnate Marshall Field II spoke on race relations. Field felt it should be handled without fanfare and as an example, referred to one of Caniff's strips in which Negro GI's had appeared. "I didn't intend to 'ram home' the race issue," Caniff explains. "I had heard that some of the soldiers working on the Burma Road were Negro. And I put them in the strip simply as a matter of fact." . . .

If all the Negro characters—minus the stereotypes—that ever made the comics were added up they still would not be enough to counter the charge that Negroes have been sorely neglected in the strips. A change in policy, while forthcoming, has not been strong enough to make a difference. And as far as many readers, cartoonists and editors are concerned, no major breakthrough is in sight.

When the facts are sifted, who can be blamed for not having Negroes in the strips? The cartoonists who draw them? The syndicates who sell them? Newspapers who buy them?

What Do You Think?

1.   Are cartoonists and editors guilty of discriminating against black people?
2.   Should an editor be considered prejudiced if he refused to run *Wee Pals* because it might hurt business?
3.   Who really determines whether a paper will discriminate or not?

ACTIVITIES FOR INVOLVEMENT

1.   Discrimination against minority races within established organizations (such as banks, local, state, or federal agencies, or unions) has been defined as "institutional racism." Such discrimination often takes place because regulations, educational requirements, or traditions exist, over which individuals by themselves have little or no control. Counselors in schools, for example, know that IQ tests do not measure fairly the intelligence of minority students, yet they often rely on the results of such tests as a guide for placing students in "slow" or "average" classes. Review the readings in this chapter to see if any examples of institutional racism are presented or suggested. List any other examples of such racism that you know of, and then prepare a second list suggesting ways by which this condition might be eliminated or reduced.

2.   The second article in this chapter describes a "double standard" being applied by a judge in his evaluations of teen-age activity. Double standards exist when the same action is excused for one group of people yet frowned on for another group. Listed below are several groups between which such double standards have been applied:

   a. Males—Females.
   b. Parents—Children.
   c. Employers—Workers.
   d. Teachers—Students.

Hold a class discussion to identify some of the double standards which exist between these groups. When, if ever, are such double standards called for? Explain.

3.   A chief complaint of many minority groups has been that of police harassment. Invite a police officer to visit your class and discuss the question of police relations with minority groups. Get ready for the visit beforehand by preparing questions like the following to ask your visitor:

   a. What effect can police have on minority relations?
   b. What laws or regulations must the policeman obey in performing investigations and in making arrests?
   c. Why are many minority groups suspicious of the police?
   d. How might relations between police and minority groups be improved?

Then ask a representative from several minority groups to visit the class and ask them the same or similar questions. How do the different speakers' answers compare? In what ways are they similar? Different? How would you explain these similarities and differences?

4.   Plan and carry on a series of activities (e.g., folk dances, film showings, music hours, human-rights poster displays, United Nations days, and the like) to draw attention within your school and/or your community to the contributions of minority groups to the culture of the United States.

5.   Develop an audio-visual presentation (using sketches, slides, cartoons, tapes, etc.) to emphasize a particular point brought out in this chapter with which you agree or disagree.

6.   Visit a local bookstore to make a two-week survey of the comic

strips in several newspapers. What evidence can you find to support or refute the views presented in Reading 9 in this chapter?

7.   A frequent statement made by individuals of minority groups is that they are constantly made to *feel* inferior. For one week, keep a personal account of the times that you have been made to feel inferior or superior to others. Try to jot down exactly *how* you felt—that is, what your feelings were at the time. Then hold a class discussion on what kinds of experiences tend to decrease one's sense of self-worth. What kinds of experiences would *increase* one's self-esteem? How might we bring more of such experiences about?

What Causes Prejudice and Discrimination?

To what extent do fear and hate cause prejudice and discrimination? What factors create attitudes and stereotypes which are accepted without challenge generation after generation? Can these traditional attitudes be changed? To what degree is ignorance at the base of prejudice? Will truth and greater knowledge reduce prejudice and discrimination?

While the following articles each emphasize a major cause, keep in mind the idea that prejudice and discrimination are usually the product of multiple causes.

1. ANTI-SEMITISM IN EUROPE *

Six million Jews were murdered in Europe during World War II. How could this happen? Could it happen in the United States?

Anti-Semitism in Germany After World War I

In the 1890's when the use of anti-Semitism as a political device was common in Germany and even more common in Austria, a young Austrian came to Vienna. There he saw a frankly anti-Semitic party win two-thirds of the seats on the city council and witnessed the political manipula-

---

* Excerpted from Milton J. Yinger, *Anti-Semitism: A Case Study in Prejudice and Discrimination.* New York, N. Y.: Anti-Defamation League, 1964. Abridgment of pp. 221–223 *Racial and Cultural Minorities* by George Eaton Simpson and J. Milton Zinger. Copyright 1953 by Harper & Row, Publishers, Incorporated. Copyright © 1958, 1965 by George Eaton Simpson and J. Milton Yinger. Reprinted by permission of Harper & Row, Publishers.

tions of anti-Semitism by Karl Lueger, who for fourteen years was burgomaster of the city. Lueger's anti-Semitism ". . . was an open anti-liberal platform device. His pupil really set out to destroy physically those whom his master so constantly taught him to regard as the most danger-ous enemies of the German people." We shall not undertake to analyze the personality basis for Hitler's anti-Semitism. Apparently he had an overpowering need for a prejudice that would allow him to thrust off his frustrations and would "explain" a complex conflict situation. It may well be that a rigid, authoritarian upbringing had created in him a self-splitting need for the contradictory feelings of dependency and domina-tion described by Eric Fromm in *Escape from Freedom.* The important thing about Nazi anti-Semitism is not the personality of Hitler but the millions of times these same personality needs were repeated, for what-ever reasons, in other Germans (and in people of many other lands)—and the tremendous impetus given to the growth of those needs by the utter disorganization of the postwar period.

Even widespread personality tendencies, however, cannot account for the Nazi movement. Why did they coalesce into a social movement? What aspects of German tradition, social structure, and societal conflict prepared the way for Nazism instead of some alternative form of ex-pression of those tendencies?

The masses did not ask for anti-Semitism, they wanted hate. They did not ask for the racial doctrine, they wanted to feel superior. They did not ask for the legend of the "stab in the back," they desired to rid themselves of what they felt to be a national humiliation. They did not demand the leader principle, but they wanted once more to obey instead of making their own decisions.

[This] statement perhaps minimizes the anti-Semitic potential in the Ger-many of the 1920's, but it helpfully suggests that the final result was not simply the consequence of individual prejudices. These were drawn upon as resources by a revolutionary movement. They must be seen against a tradition of anti-Semitism that reaches back hundreds of years. In his detailed account of the Nazi policy of extermination, Hilberg notes the precedents of discrimination, stereotypy, and violence—even if not of genocide—in medieval Canon law, in the writings of Martin Luther, and in later German history. . . . To this we must add, as background influences: military defeat, after four years of bitter war; the loss of colonies and homeland territory; the Versailles Treaty with its "guilt clause"; the political conflict of the left and right (with the Weimar Republic, in between, being torn to pieces); and the utter confusion of the [economic] inflation. These so enlarged the group of the hopeless, cynical, and con-fused that the basis was laid for the development of a strong anti-Semitic movement. . . .

Perhaps the most skillful use of anti-Semitism by Hitler was the way he won the support—or at least held off the opposition—of some of the most powerful industrial and military figures of Germany by making communism seem to be a Jewish product. This idea also appealed to many members of the middle class, who identified themselves with the old regime in opposition to the urban proletariat. A traditional prejudice can be played upon in such a way that judgment is thoroughly lost, when the will to believe is strong. Only one out of eighty-nine Communist members of the 1932 Reichstag was a Jew; there were only 600,000 Jews in Germany, but the Communists received almost six million votes —yet Nazi propaganda was able to link the Jews with communism in many people's minds.

Thus Hitler used anti-Semitism to forge a superficial unity out of intrinsically contradictory appeals. The basis had been laid in *Mein Kampf* where he developed a theory of history that solves, at one blow, all the complicated problems with which modern social science works. Success and failure, the good and bad are all to be explained by race:

"Everything that today we admire on this earth—science and art, technique and inventions—is only the creative product of a few peoples and perhaps originally of one race. On them now depends also the existence of this entire culture. If they perish, then the beauty of this earth sinks into the grave with them.

"The blood-mixing . . . is the sole cause of the dying-off of old cultures."

Starting from this premise that race is the most important thing in the world, Hitler developed his conception of the Jews and their role in Germany's problems. He distinguished three types of races: the culture-founders, the culture-bearers, and the culture-destroyers. Only "Aryans" are culture-founders; some other "races" are culture-bearers, although their role is precarious, depending upon contact with the superior Aryans; but Jews, said Hitler, are culture-destroyers. He pictured them simultaneously as weak and cowardly yet enormously powerful and dangerous, giving his followers a sense of fear, but then a way to escape their fear—if they will follow him. The mutually contradictory qualities in these stereotypes are no obstacle for those ready to believe and needing a security-giving formula.

If the Jews were alone in this world, they would suffocate as much in dirt and filth, as they would carry on a detestable struggle to cheat and ruin each other, although the complete lack of the will to sacrifice, expressed in their cowardice, would also in this instance make the fight a comedy.

If we let all the causes of the German collapse pass before our eyes, there remains as the ultimate and decisive cause the nonrecognition of the race problem and especially of the Jewish danger.

Using that kind of doctrine as rationalization, the Nazis launched the most extensive and bloody campaign against the Jews that the world has ever seen. A few items will illustrate the cumulative attack on the very existence of the Jews. In 1933 a new civil service law dismissed all "non-Aryan" officials, excepting ex-servicemen or those who held their jobs before August 1, 1914. This affected teachers, university professors, judges, public prosecutors, as well as the staffs of government bureaus. Non-Aryan lawyers were debarred and non-Aryan doctors deprived of their panel practice, with the same exceptions. In 1934 the "Aryan clause" was adopted by the army. In 1935 the Nuremberg laws deprived all Jews of citizenship and therefore eliminated all exceptions to the employment of Jewish officials that previous decrees had allowed. In 1936 the expropriation of Jewish-owned firms without compensation began. On November 10, 1938, an anti-Jewish pogrom started simultaneously in all German towns; all Jewish stores were demolished and thousands of Jews arrested. Jews were then required to repair all the damage; they forfeited any insurance claims to the government and were fined, collectively, about 400 million dollars (one billion marks). On February 25, 1939, the Jewish community of Berlin was given orders to produce daily the names of one hundred persons who were to receive two weeks' notice to leave the country.

After the outbreak of World War II and the extension of German domination over most of Europe, any restraints that still protected the Jews were abandoned. The Nazis systematically overworked, starved, and murdered the Jews in every land they occupied. The outside world could scarcely believe the reports of the slaughter until German records brought into the Nuremberg trials after the war, gave conclusive evidence. By 1945 the Nazis had killed six million Jews. Before the war there were over three million Jews in Poland; today there are only 32,000. At the end of the war scarcely ten thousand of the Jewish population of Germany remained. To the personal violence of the Crusades and the planned violence of the czarist regime the Nazis added a technological violence that virtually destroyed the Jewish population of Europe outside of Russia. Perhaps a million escaped (to Russia, Palestine, the United States, Latin America, and elsewhere); perhaps a million are yet alive in Europe (not including Great Britain and the Soviet Union); but six million were killed.

The brutality of the campaign of annihilation of European Jews is almost beyond comprehension. Lest we assume, however, that this somehow sets the Germans apart as altogether depraved, we ought to note that the capacity for violence and torture—or indifference to these things in others—is, most tragically, widely shared.

Anti-Semitism in Europe After World War II

The defeat of Nazism and the virtual destruction of European Jewry removed anti-Semitism as a major political force in Europe. It did not, however, mean the disappearance of anti-Semitism from Europe. In the summer of 1949 the voters of West Germany held their first free election since 1933. Parties that were rather frankly ultranationalistic, pro-Nazi, and anti-Semitic received a vote variously estimated at from three to six millions, out of a total of twenty-five million votes. Since then, political anti-Semitism has faded. There remain scattered acts of violence, vandalism against synagogues, publication of anti-Semitic pamphlets, and the expression of some Nazi sentiments. Other countries of Western Europe exhibit similar tendencies. This is particularly true of France, where remnants of her war-time regime, deep-seated political conflicts, and the migration of over 100,000 Algerian Jews combine to maintain a potentially difficult anti-Semitic situation. In other parts of the world, those countries with strong European ties experience persistent, even if minor, anti-Semitic outbreaks. This is perhaps most true of Argentina.

In Eastern Europe and the Soviet Union anti-Semitism continues to be used on occasion as a weapon of government.

Nearly one-quarter of the world's 12 and a half million Jews live in the Soviet Union (estimates range from 2.2 to 3.0 million). Against the background of generations of violence in pre-Soviet days and an official policy of non-discrimination today, we see a pattern of prejudice and attacks on the equal rights of Jews that seems designed both to use them as scapegoats and to destroy them as a distinctive ethnic group. The study of Hebrew is prohibited, religious objects cannot be made, and virtually no religious literature has been published. No Jewish leader has been allowed to have official contact with Jews in other lands. . . .

Despite the defeat of Nazism, therefore, and despite the revulsion against its ideology and policies, we may not have seen the end of anti-Semitism, even of the organized and political type, in Europe and in the Soviet Union. Individual frustration focused by a traditional prejudice and the presumed usefulness of a scapegoat in internal and international affairs keep it alive.

What Do You Think?

1. In light of the Jewish experience in Europe, to what extent does an individual determine whether or not he will be prejudiced or discriminate against his fellow man?

2. Are there conditions in the U. S. today that some people might like to explain by the simple process of scapegoating?

3. What does the Jewish experience under the Nazi regime suggest about the causes of prejudice and discrimination?

2. THE DAY I LEARNED ABOUT PREJUDICE *

In the following article a family is destroyed because it was different. What is it that causes people to react to the unknown, the different, in such a violent fashion?

As I walked along the dusty sidewalk toward home, swiping at the sweat running down my face, my pinafore limp in the still heat, I played a wishing game. I was wishing the trouble in town would go away.

There was a strike on among the miners. Ordinarily a rough but kindly lot, the continuing strike was making them nervous and resentful, restless with inactivity. Now the strike had been complicated, its direction changed by the inexplicable murder of two little girls who had been friends. No one knew who the murderer was. Within a short time, suspicion and distrust spread, and the "native" Americans were pitted against the "foreign-born." Reason disappeared as people tormented one another with name-calling. The least excuse served for violence. Attempts by the authorities to discover the truth were fruitless, and rumors began to be accepted as fact.

Two days before at our house we had celebrated my brother Sandy's fifth birthday, but it hadn't been much of a celebration—not with the police trucks rumbling past, stirring up the dry road so that the dust filtered through the screens of the open windows and settled all over Sandy's cake.

Oddly, this afternoon there didn't seem to be any trucks or police around. A strange quiet lay over Tenth Street, a quiet that made me glance uneasily behind, as if someone might be stealing up to grab me. A door banged along the street, empty of children and women, empty even of the few automobiles that customarily jogged along it to town. . . .

Then, down the way in the direction from which I had come, I heard another bang. A man appeared from somewhere, but I couldn't see which door had closed behind him. Another man joined him. Two came from the alley and walked behind them. The miners didn't greet each other, the way people usually did—just went along as though they were angry. Five other men from various spots fell in line with the four, all

* Excerpted from "The Day I Learned About Prejudice," Eula A. Morrison, in *Mademoiselle;* copyright © 1966 by The Condé Nast Publications, Inc.

shambling in a half march behind me. More swung in from here and there.

I began running. I felt an urgency to keep ahead of them. My breath began coming in gasps, then whistles. My chest started hurting; black specks danced ahead of me as I turned dizzy from the heat. Still, I dared not stop running.

Our house came in sight, its gray and white paint beginning to dull beneath the onslaught of soot that bathed it daily. Home had always been a refuge in which to recover from whatever hurt or frightened me in the world outside. I was frightened now without knowing why.

As I ran to our sidewalk, I heard voices. Looking up, I saw Mother and the mayor's wife sitting behind the partially closed front porch. They were sewing and talking. Mother, a widowed schoolteacher, spent summer vacations making our clothes.

I heard Mother say, "If we taught our children to try to understand others, the Hammars wouldn't have to hide." I stumbled over an uneven section of cement and Mother glanced my way, breaking off. "Why, honey," she called, "don't you know better than to run like that on such a hot day?"

"I—" I looked over my shoulder. The men were scuffling determinedly along, closing the distance between me and them.

Mother's glance followed mine. Wordless, she rose and studied the silent group. Then, laying her sewing aside, she said, "Mrs. Coxley, I think there's going to be trouble of some kind. You'd better call your husband. He can get in touch with the police." To me, she said, "Go inside—and see that Sandy stays with you." . . .

There was something horrible about that silent trotting bunch. They went past our place, past the Hammars'—deserted since the Hammars had been frightened away by a threatening letter—past all the houses until they reached the corner. I lost sight of them as they turned.

Mrs. Coxley called on a note of hysteria, "The telephone's dead! I can't get Mr. Coxley—I can't get anyone!"

"Then we'd better find another telephone," Mother said in a calming voice. "I'm afraid that mob's going to a certain—"

"The Patricellis', I bet!" I burst out. "Ange's papa said he wouldn't be scared away by no one. Kids say Mr. Patricelli's got a still—in his cellar." Mother turned, her face paling. "A still's as good an excuse for that mob as any," she said tautly. . . .

"Where's Sandy?" Mother asked then.

Aghast, my face screwed up with panic. Without replying, I sprinted through the living room to the back of the house, calling him. There was no answer. Mother joined me in the kitchen, having made a tour of the rooms herself.

"Look out back, and around the Hammars' place," she commanded. . . .

Not telling Mother what I feared, I hurried through our backyard, through the vacant one of the Hammars. I raced to where the men had turned earlier. The Patricellis lived a street over. As I rounded the corner, I heard a muttering. There was an animal snarl to it, that, from a distance, reminded me of dogs growling before a fight. And there, skipping along, was Sandy, his body bent forward in an excited way, his face turned toward the muttering men.

"Sandy!" I called. "Come home!"

There was taunting now, angry taunting: "Yah-yah!" "Foreigners!"

I gathered an extra burst of speed; or maybe the narrowing of the distance between us was due to Sandy's reaching the edge of the mob and stopping to stare wonderingly at the men.

There was a rise in the sidewalk, and I paused to get my breath while surveying the area below. And I thought Sandy might see me on the higher ground. As I watched, the crowd surrounded the Patricelli house, milling past a woodpile outside the kitchen door. Chips, freshly cut, lay on the ground, and an ax stuck up from a chunk of wood, its blade sunk deep in the grain.

The shattering of glass, the squeezing forward of the mob, as if it would press out the people in the house by sheer weight of numbers, sent me tearing downhill. There was a shouted, "Patricelli! Come out! Murderer!"

As I ran, a rock hit another window, and the shrill cry of a woman rose above the sound. "Go 'way!" she screamed. "Go 'way! He not here!"

A movement on the front porch drew my glance. Mrs. Patricelli came from the doorway to the railing, a baby in her arms. Everyone knew it was only three days old. Now, Mrs. Patricelli was standing there, weak and white-faced, staring defiantly at the crowd. Huddled against her side was Ange, sister to the baby, her face set with fear.

I was only a few feet from Sandy now, and as I called to him he half-turned. But then another window broke. At the same time, as if at some signal, the mob surged forward. The men streamed up the steps, pushing Mrs. Patricelli aside, and poured into the house. High above that angry clamor, Mrs. Patricelli was crying, "No! No!"

As I hurried forward, frantically trying to reach Sandy, Mrs. Patricelli ran to the sidewalk, Ange with her, the baby crying. Then I heard Sandy yelling my name from behind the woodpile.

Forgetting Mrs. Patricelli and the new baby, forgetting everything except that Sandy must be got away from there, I leapt over the wood chunks and grabbed his hand. I had him at my side with a jerk, then clambered back the way I had come, dragging him in haste, trying to get away from some horror I sensed waiting to engulf the place. . . .

Suddenly there was something like a chuckle behind us, not a merry sound, but chilling. I looked around. The mob was spilling out the back way. High on someone's shoulders was a man. He was handed from one shoulder to another, never falling to the ground. Mrs. Patricelli ran toward them, with Ange still holding to her skirts. "He do no wrong!" Mrs. Patricelli was crying.

The ax that had been sticking up in the chunk of wood gleamed in the sunlight as it was lifted high in the air, its blade above the heads of the men, above Mrs. Patricelli, above her husband. Then, as though wielded by an invisible hand, the ax came down.

A hush, an odd lack of movement where so much movement had been, came over the men. The low despairing cry of Mrs. Patricelli was clear in that stillness.

"My man! They've killed my man—"

Sick, terrified, I put an arm around Sandy and stumbled home.

A few weeks later the real murderer of the two children was discovered.

What Do You Think?

1. To what extent was fear important in triggering the violent death of Mr. Patricelli? Explain.
2. Why did the mob choose the Patricelli family?
3. Could an incident such as the one described happen today? Why or why not?

3. BLACK RAGE *

The authors see prejudice and discrimination against Negroes as an outgrowth of the relationship between slave and master. Is it possible that a condition over a hundred years in the past can affect the behavior of people today?

The black man of today is at one end of a psychological continuum which reaches back in time to his enslaved ancestors. Observe closely a man on a Harlem street corner and it can be seen how little his life experience differs from that of his forebears. However much the externals differ, their inner life is remarkably the same.

On a cold morning one of the authors sat watching a group of black men. They were standing outside an office for casual laborers in clusters of four or five. A truck drove up and they stiffened. There was

---

* Excerpted from William H. Grier and Price M. Cobbs, *Black Rage*. New York, N. Y.: Basic Books, Inc., 1968.

a ripple of excitement as a white man leaned out of the cab and squinted. As he ran his eyes past the different men, one could almost hear his thoughts.

This one is too thin . . . that dark one looks smart-alecky and is probably slow . . . the boy way in the back there might do.

No imagination is required to see this scene as a direct remnant of slavery. Move back in time and this could be an auction block. The manual labor is the same and so is the ritual of selection. The white man involved in the selection feels he is only securing a crew. But, then, so did his forefathers. In addition, the psychic structure of the black men being selected has altered little since slavery. To know this is deeply troubling—and frightening.

A city erupts in fury. Its residents are appalled and outraged. Biracial committees are appointed and scapegoats appear from everywhere. Instead of wretched housing and stifling unemployment, outside agitators and wily Communists are said to be the most important causes. Always the basic reasons are at best minimized and at worst denied. After three centuries of oppression the black man is still thought to need a provocateur to inflame him!

History is forgotten. There is little record of the first Africans brought to this country. They were stripped of everything. A calculated cruelty was begun, designed to crush their spirit. After they were settled in the white man's land, the malice continued. When slavery ended and large-scale physical abuse was discontinued, it was supplanted by different but equally damaging abuse. The cruelty continued unabated in thoughts, feelings, intimidation, and occasional lynching. Black people were consigned to a place outside the human family and the whip of the plantation was replaced by the boundaries of the ghetto.

The culture of slavery was never undone for either master or slave. The civilization that tolerated slavery dropped its slaveholding cloak but the inner feelings remained. The "peculiar institution" continues to exert its evil influence over the nation. The practice of slavery stopped over a hundred years ago, but the minds of our citizens have never been freed.

What Do You Think?

1. Do you agree with the authors' conclusion that the labor selection incident represented "a direct remnant of slavery"?
2. What might be a slave owner's attitude toward slaves *before* they were freed? What might the slave owner's son's attitudes toward slaves be after they were freed?
3. Would you agree that "the minds of our citizens have never been freed" of slavery?

4. PREJUDICE IN THE SUBURBS *

Religions have consistently been a target for prejudice and discrimination. Here is how Marty Stewart, a bright, good-looking, popular teenager feels about her religion. What do her remarks suggest about the causes of prejudice?

I am Jewish. Being a Jew means quite a lot to me, and I would never change my religion. It is not that I think other religions are inferior, but I feel that my religion is the best for me. It helps to guide me through the obstacles that I encounter in my life. Among these obstacles are incidents where I have come upon prejudice aimed towards me.

These little incidents, slips of the tongue, or commonly used expressions, seem small; but they inflict such great pain. I'm really very sorry that people should see fit to use such terms as "kike," "you Jew," or "Jew you out." People seem to think of the stereotyped Jew who hoards his money and lends it out at a high interest rate. They seem to be unaware that during the Renaissance the Jews were forced into becoming money lenders. They were not allowed to do much else. They could not become "honorable professionals" such as doctors and lawyers.

Many people feel "every Jew is a bad Jew" just as they feel "every Negro is a bad Negro." Some people refuse to accept Jews as people. One thing like that happened to my parents when they first came to California. One of the first couples that my parents met was anti-Semitic. They didn't know that my parents were Jewish. They accepted them and liked them. When they found out that our family was Jewish, they were amazed that Jewish people could be so nice. They've been best friends ever since.

One other thing that just fries me is when somebody says to me with his mouth open and eyes wide, "You're Jewish? You don't look it!" Just what is a Jew supposed to look like? Not every Jew has long side ringlets and a large nose.

Such assumptions and generalizations are ruinous to our society. I don't blame anyone, I blame society. A child who grows up in an environment where people hate another race or creed is bound to grow up with these same prejudices. No one is born with prejudice; they accumulate it.

Society seems to condone segregation—take country clubs, for example. I once was dating a boy whose father belonged to a country club

---

* By Marty Stewart, Hillsborough, Calif.

in a fairly wealthy area. I expressed a wish to see this place, so he took me there. As we entered the door he whispered to me, "You know, if they knew you were here, they'd kick you out." You can't imagine my humiliation and my anger. I felt crushed and slighted; yet at the same time I felt proud. Now why I felt this, I don't know. Maybe it's because I'm not ashamed of my religion. I'm proud of it, and I'm proud to be a Jew.

One day when I was visiting my relatives back in my home state, Illinois, my cousins and a friend of theirs took me driving and showed me the sights of their city. As we went by the Jewish Temple, their friend turned to me and said, "There's the Jews' place. All the rich Jews who came from Chicago live there." Then he said jokingly, "I hope you're not Jewish." Then he laughed. You should have seen his face when I said, "Yes, I am." Boy, he sure apologized fast! He was so embarrassed, and I can't blame him. But this just shows what kind of generalizations people make and how they form their opinions of people before they even know them.

And one last thing. I'd like to talk about a particular time in class when we were talking about German government in World War II. I almost cried—and did later. The teacher didn't mean to question me about the Jews in Germany, only about authoritarian government. Yet, I froze and couldn't answer. It wasn't what he said that made me feel so badly; it was the people in the class. They all seemed to be glaring at me. They know I'm Jewish; I made no attempt to hide it, and maybe that's wrong. Anyway, I heard them say to themselves, "Boy, who does she think she is? After all, she's Jewish and just as prejudiced as the Nazis." I then remembered times when my Christian "friends" would talk to me about my religion and how they thought I was so queer. I also heard people in class go "tsk, tsk," or clicking the roof of their mouths with their tongues like they were disgusted with me. It was then that I just couldn't hold on any longer. That's why I couldn't speak; why, if I had, I would have started to cry right there. I know I shouldn't be so sensitive, but I'm sick and tired of being persecuted, of being thought different. I'm disgusted with people who use phrases like, "You Jew" and the like. I'm sick of the whole thing. But I know I must live with it, for people will never be able to understand one another. They are too complex and too concerned with the image of society. There will always be a scapegoat. And as long as there are minority groups around, they will be persecuted and treated unjustly.

What Do You Think?

1. What does Marty Stewart think is the cause of prejudice and discrimination?

2.   What does Marty Stewart mean when she says, "There will always be a scapegoat"?

3.   Do you feel Marty Stewart is oversensitive to her Jewishness?

5.   ONE LITTLE BOY MEETS PREJUDICE *

Prejudice may be directed against anyone. This black mother attempted to teach her young child about prejudice. What does she indicate to be some of its causes?

No child is born with prejudice. Prejudice is something he catches like mumps or measles. Whether the prejudice is against race, religion, color, creed or national origin, the pattern is the same; the child takes his attitudes from his family and his friends.

So often prejudice is described in terms of white children learning to discriminate against children of other races and colors. But prejudice works both ways. . . .

Meet Jimmy, a ten-year-old. All his life this youngster has spent much of his time with people of various races, colors and creeds. His friends include Jews and Gentiles, refugees and other white families and American Negro families. He was almost five before he heard the term "white people." It happened this way.

One Sunday, while looking over the housing section of the paper, he remarked, "These are white people's houses." "Who are white people?" we asked him. "People who live in white houses," he answered seriously. When asked what made people white, he answered impatiently, "They are white because they live in white houses."

It was a year later before he ventured another comment about race. A relative was powdering her nose and he objected, saying that it made her look white. Then he added in a matter-of-fact way. "I don't like white people." I named one of his godparents, asking if he liked him. "Oh sure!" When I said, "Well, he is white," the boy stared at me in disbelief, assuring me that he could not be white. The same reaction occurred as I named various white friends he liked. Finally he accepted my statement, but said in a puzzled way: "I didn't know they were white."

At six, he heard from friends at school that one does not like white people and he had taken on this prejudice without quite being able to understand the difference in skin color. He was confused at learning that some people he liked were white but at the end of the discussion, he was willing to qualify his statement to "Well, I don't like some white people." He could not say why he disliked any of them.

---

* Excerpted from "One Little Boy Meets Prejudice," Ophelia Settle Egypt, *Parents Magazine,* February 1956.

Four months later, he watched a fight between white and Negro boys and heard the discussion which followed among his friends. One of his pals made the statement that white people are "mean," and my son repeated it, adding that he wished a certain boy was white so he could fight him. Here he had taken on a generalization growing out of actual observation of a racial clash. He had identified himself for the first time as different from white people and as a member of the Negro group. As such a member, he could categorize the whole opposite group as mean, and draw the conclusion that it was all right to fight a white boy but not a member of his own group.

Again I named some of his favorite white friends, asking if they were mean, and in each case received an emphatic no. His pal then said firmly that some white people are mean, but others are all right. Then he added, "But I wouldn't go to a white person's house." Parrot-like my son declared he wouldn't either. When asked if they remembered the party they went to at a friend's home, they began to talk enthusiastically about it. They had such a good time. When they paused in their enthusiatic review of the visit, I remarked casually that they had been in a white person's house then, that all of the people there were white. They decided then that these friends of theirs were "okay" and agreed that it was all right to visit their homes, but they were still skeptical about unknown white people.

In other words mere association with people who are different in skin color does not necessarily prevent a young child from taking on the prejudice of his associates. The normal desire of an individual to be "like" rather than "different," often closes his eyes to the differences in others. . . .

It may strike some parents as strange that the next step in this child's thinking was related to the difference in color within his own race. One day, on his return from school, out of a clear sky came the statement, "I'm glad I'm brown because I don't like black people." Again the process of discussion, calling attention to his friends who would be considered black, led him to the conclusion that skin color isn't really important. He began to realize that he was merely repeating what he had heard, and at seven he began to evaluate his friends' statements more carefully and think for himself. Now, his best friend is darker than he.

If a parent is unprejudiced, the child has a greater opportunity to learn to accept other people as they are. However, group forces outside the home are strong influences, and group methods of combatting prejudice are equally important. A child cannot bear to be different from his play group; therefore such heroes as Bill Cosby and Dick Gregory can do much to mold the attitudes of the group. Bible classes also prove effective when the principle of the brotherhood of man is made realistic for the child. . . .

And underneath it all there must be a firm belief in a living democracy if one would help a child to learn that prejudice, whether based on race, religion, or national origin, is untenable.

What Do You Think?

1. Was Jimmy's mother's work a wasted effort? Explain your thinking.
2. Would Bill Cosby and Dick Gregory be important images for a boy like Jimmy? Explain.

6. THE SOCIAL PSYCHOLOGY OF ANTI-SEMITISM *

Do you think about minorities in the same way your friends do? If you moved to a different city and your new friends were prejudiced, would you become prejudiced?

There have been many attempts to discover whether certain occupational groups, classes, regions, or personality types are likely to be more anti-Semitic than others. Not all individuals or groups are equally susceptible to anti-Semitic beliefs or actions. The results of studies seeking to isolate the factors that predispose an individual to acceptance of this prejudice are somewhat contradictory, but it is well to examine them to discover the degree of agreement and to make clear that any easy explanation is impossible. They point to the need for distinguishing carefully among the various kinds of anti-Semitism (from sharing the verbal stereotypes to active discrimination) and for continuing analysis of the many different roots of anti-Semitism.

Harlan asked 502 college students (from three southern and one northern school) to check their degree of agreement or disagreement with twelve brief stories that described pro- or anti-Jewish behavior. He found, as most studies do, that women are less prejudiced than men. Students whose home residences were in larger communities were more preju-

---

* Excerpted from Milton J. Yinger, *Anti-Semitism: A Case Study in Prejudice and Discrimination.* New York, N. Y.: Anti-Defamation League, 1964. Abridgment of pp. 209–212 *Racial and Cultural Minorities* by George Eaton Simpson and J. Milton Yinger. Copyright 1953 by Harper & Row, Publishers, Incorporated. Copyright © 1958, 1965 by George Eaton Simpson and J. Milton Yinger. Reprinted by permission of Harper & Row, Publishers.

diced than those from smaller communities. Students whose parents were engaged in business or professional occupations were more prejudiced than those from the homes of skilled workers, farmers, or clerical workers. Prejudice varied directly with income; the higher the income of the family, the more the prejudice. It also varied directly with frequency of contact with Jews, even when two groups were compared that had been matched for region, size of home community, income, sex ratio, and number of Jewish friends. And finally, it varied inversely with the number of intimate Jewish friends; those without them were most prejudiced. The probability that differences as large as those found, for example, between high and low income groups could be due simply to chance is less than one in a hundred.

These data would seem to indicate that persons likely to be in most direct competition with Jews and those who are most likely to oppose social change (because they receive high rewards in the existing situation) are most anti-Semitic, as measured by Harlan's type of scale. When date of study, region, and type of question are changed, however, the results may vary. In 1958, the American Institute of Public Opinion asked a cross section of the American population this question: "If your party nominated a generally well-qualified man for President, and he happened to be a Jew, would you vote for him?" Those answering "yes," were divided into the following four educational levels:

Grade School	59%
Some high school	68%
Completed high school	69%
College	82%

It is important to recognize the limitations and weaknesses of this kind of measurement. Anti-Semitism must be defined, in this context, as willingness to make the verbal responses that have been designated as anti-Semitic by the poll taker. Responses to a different question often indicate different results. For example, a *Fortune* poll in October, 1947, using a secret ballot, found, contrary to the data above, that a larger proportion of farmers and residents of small towns than residents of cities thought Jews had "too much say in government." This result must be qualified, however, by the fact that the city vote contained a much higher proportion of Jewish respondents. It may also measure simply the response to a stereotype, not readiness to engage in overt anti-Semitic activity; or, more specifically, it may measure a stereotype only in the field of politics.

Another difference in the results of various measures of anti-Semitism is shown in the data on regional variation. In 1946, Roper found from a sample of adults that respondents in the Northeast and Middle West made or accepted more anti-Semitic statements than those from the South and West. Harlan found the same thing in his college sample;

students from the North showed more prejudice than those from the South. In 1949, however, Roper interviewed a cross section of 1000 freshmen and 1000 seniors on fifty different campuses and found southern students to be the most anti-Semitic. Owing to the greater adequacy of his sampling procedure, Roper's measure of prejudice among students must be accepted as the more reliable; but the differences indicate the need for caution in our judgments. . . .

An intensive study of 150 veterans in Chicago revealed a number of significant relationships between personal and group characteristics and anti-Semitism in this largely lower-middle-class group. On the basis of exploratory interviews with a small group of veterans not included in the final sample, Bettelheim and Janowitz developed a classification of four types of veterans according to their attitudes toward Jews:

1. The *intensely anti-Semitic* veteran was spontaneously outspoken in expressing a preference for restrictive action against the Jews even before the subject was raised. For example, he might have advocated Hitler's solution to the Jewish problem here in America, when asked whether there were any groups of people trying to get ahead at his expense. When questioned directly about the Jews, he maintained his outspoken preference for restrictive action. For example, he might have objected to having Jews as next-door neighbors, to working on the same job with them, or he might have advocated prevention of inter-marriage with Jews. Finally he also displayed a wide range of unfavorable stereotyped opinions about the Jews.

2. The *outspokenly anti-Semitic* veteran revealed no spontaneous preference for restrictive action against the Jews. Instead, outspoken hostility toward the Jews emerged only toward the end of the interview when he was questioned directly. As in the case of the intensely anti-Semitic veteran, his thinking contained a wide range of unfavorable stereotypes.

3. The *stereotyped anti-Semitic* veteran expressed no preference for hostile or restrictive action against the Jews, either spontaneously or when questioned directly. Instead, he merely expressed a variety of stereotyped notions about the Jews, including some which were not necessarily unfavorable from his point of view. For example, he might have thought Jews clannish, or that they are people who engage in shrewd business methods. But he felt, for any number of reasons, that these characteristics did not justify aggressive action against the Jews, by the government or by society at large.

4. The *tolerant* veteran revealed no elaborate stereotyped beliefs about the Jews although even the most tolerant veterans expressed isolated stereotypes from time to time. Moreover,

neither spontaneously nor when questioned directly, did he advocate restrictive action against the Jews. In fact, on policy questions, the tolerant person either denied any just grounds for differentiating between Jews and non-Jews, or affirmed his lack of concern about such differences.

When the 150 men in the study were classified on the basis of these types, the following distribution resulted:

	DISTRIBUTION OF ANTI-SEMITISM		DISTRIBUTION OF ANTI-NEGRO ATTITUDES	
	Number	Percent	Number	Percent
Tolerant	61	41	12	8
Stereotyped	42	28	40	27
Outspoken	41	27	74	49
Intense	6	4	24	16
Total	150	100	150	100

For purposes of comparison, attitudes toward the Negro, based on the same classification, are also given. For the most part, as intolerance toward the Jew increased, even greater intolerance toward the Negro was exhibited. There was only one case in which tolerance toward the Negro was accompanied by outspoken anti-Semitism.

By what personal and group characteristics were the tolerant veterans distinguished from the intolerant? An answer to this question helps to reveal the causes of anti-Semitism. The authors thought that the children of European immigrants might show more prejudice than those of native-born parents, since anti-Semitism had been so strong in parts of Europe. This assumption did not prove to be true. There was a difference, too small to be statistically significant, between children of mixed parentage (one parent foreign-born) and those whose parents were both native or both foreign-born. Subjects who had one native and one foreign-born parent were somewhat more intolerant of both Jews and Negroes. It is a tenable hypothesis—only suggested, not substantiated by this study—that persons brought up in mixed families felt less family cohesion and therefore experienced a greater insecurity that led to aggression.

What Do You Think?

1. Why should college students be less anti-Semitic than those with only an elementary school education?
2. What significance do you attach to the conclusions which show that anti-Semitism and anti-Negro attitudes often appear in the same person?

3. Many of the statistics reported in this reading are from ten to twenty years old. Would they still apply today? Why or why not?

7. THE HAPPY HOUSEWIFE HEROINE *

Some writers in the 1960's felt that women were being culturally brainwashed into accepting themselves only as housewives and mothers. Press and opinion glorified the homebody role, insisting that women were emotionally incapable of competing in the business world. (See Reading 6 in Chapter 3.) Is it possible that this stereotype is restricting women's place in the world? Betty Freidan, author of The Feminine Mystique, *explains it in this fashion.*

And so the feminine mystique [women's new stereotype] began to spread through the land, grafted onto old prejudices and comfortable conventions which so easily give the past a stranglehold on the future. . . . The feminine mystique says that the highest value and the only commitment for women is the fulfillment of their femininity. . . . The root of women's troubles in the past is that women envied men, women tried to be like men, instead of accepting their own nature, which can find fulfillment only in passivity, male domination, and nurturing maternal love.

But the new image this mystique gives to American women is the old image: "Occupation: housewife." The new mystique makes the housewife-mothers, who never had a chance to be anything else, the model for all women; it presupposes that history has reached a final and glorious end in the here and now, as far as women are concerned. Beneath the sophisticated trappings, it simply makes certain concrete, finite, domestic aspects of feminine existence—as it was lived by women whose lives were confined, by necessity, to cooking, cleaning, washing, bearing children—into a religion, a pattern by which all women must now live or deny their femininity.

Fulfillment as a woman had only one definition for American women after 1949—the housewife-mother. As swiftly as in a dream, the image of the American woman as a changing, growing individual in a changing world was shattered. Her solo flight to find her own identity was forgotten in the rush for the security of togetherness. Her limitless world shrunk to the cozy walls of home.

The transformation, reflected in the pages of the women's magazines, was sharply visible in 1949 and progressive through the fifties. "Femininity

---

* Reprinted from *The Feminine Mystique,* by Betty Friedan. By permission of W. W. Norton. Copyright © 1963 by Betty Friedan.

Begins at Home," "It's a Man's World Maybe," "Have Babies While You're Young," "How to Snare a Male," "Should I Stop Work When We Marry?" "Are You Training Your Daughter to Be a Wife?" "Careers at Home," "Do Women Have to Talk So Much?" "Why GI's Prefer Those German Girls," "What Women Can Learn from Mother Eve," "Really a Man's World, Politics," "How to Hold On to a Happy Marriage," "Don't Be Afraid to Marry Young," "The Doctor Talks About Breast-Feeding," "Our Baby Was Born at Home," "Cooking to Me Is Poetry," "The Business of Running a Home."

By the end of 1949, only one out of three heroines in the women's magazines was a career woman—and she was shown in the act of renouncing her career and discovering that what she really wanted to be was a housewife. In 1958, and again in 1959, I went through issue after issue of the three major women's magazines (the fourth, *Women's Home Companion,* had died) without finding a single heroine who had a career, a commitment to any work, art, profession, or mission in the world, other than "Occupation: housewife." Only one in a hundred heroines had a job; even the young unmarried heroines no longer worked except at snaring a husband. . . .

Here is a typical specimen from a story called "The Sandwich Maker" (*Ladies' Home Journal,* April, 1959). She took home economics in college, learned how to cook, never held a job, and still plays the child bride, though she now has three children of her own. . . .

The problem is her $42.10 allowance. She hates having to ask her husband for money every time she needs a pair of shoes, but he won't trust her with a charge account. "Oh, how I yearned for a little money of my own!" . . .

At last the solution comes—she will take orders for sandwiches from other men at her husband's plant. She earns $52.50 a week, except that she forgets to count costs, and she doesn't remember what a gross is so she has to hide 8,640 sandwich bags behind the furnace. Charley says she's making the sandwiches too fancy. She explains: "If it's only ham on rye, then I'm just a sandwich maker, and I'm not interested. But the extras, the special touches—well, they make it sort of creative." So she chops, wraps, peels, seals, spreads bread, starting at dawn and never finished, for $9.00 net, until she is disgusted by the smell of food, and finally staggers downstairs after a sleepless night to slice a salami for the eight gaping lunch boxes. "It was too much. Charley came down just then, and after one quick look at me, ran for a glass of water." She realizes that she is going to have another baby.

"Charley's first coherent words were 'I'll cancel your lunch orders. You're a mother. That's your job. You don't have to earn money too.' It was all so beautifully simple! 'Yes, boss,' I murmured obediently, frankly relieved." That night he brings her home a checkbook; he will trust her with a joint account. So she decides just to keep quiet about the 8,640 sandwich bags. Anyhow, she'll have used them up, making sandwiches for four children to take to school, by the time the youngest is ready for college.

1. Does the stereotype described by the author fit the traditional American view of woman in American society?
2. What do you think might cause a society to change its attitudes about the role that women should expect to play in the world outside the home?

8. ANGRY CHICANO SOUL *

Have you ever thought of the Western part of the U. S. as stolen property? Mexican-Americans have.

We reject the white man's subterfuge of classifying us as white, and relegating us to a second class citizenship. We reject it thoroughly; and in its place we reassert, we reaffirm our own unique culture, our own language, our own way of life. In essence—our own soul.

Now—how many of you good gringos know that you are presently living in illegally occupied Mexican territory?

Remember the term, "manifest destiny"?—The white man's euphemism invented to hide the ugly truth, the brutal reality, the true tragedy . . . That in fact you mercilessly murdered Mexicans and blatantly stole the land from Mexico. Quickly forgetting the treaty agreements, and through political manipulations, legal frauds, and out and out thievery you unjustifiably usurped the God-given land, rightfully belonging to Mexicans?

But your inhumane materialistic thirst was not satisfied with merely more land gained through murder . . . no, you then proceeded to brutalize my surviving brown brothers—
To terrorize our women and children
To castrate our culture
To destroy our destiny
To chain our Chicano soul to the land that, under your corrupt law, no longer belonged to us.
In essence, you denied us our human dignity.

We have not forgotten! Indeed, we cannot forget. And to remind

* Excerpted from Manuel Gomez, *La Hormiga,* September 12, 1968.

you, listen—Sacramento, San Francisco, San Jose, Santa Cruz, Monterey, Los Angeles, San Diego, and on and on and on . . . The history of California, and of the entire Southwest, blares out in echoing screams, the sweat, the blood, and the tears of Mexicans! Viva la Raza!

NO, we have not forgotten. For the scar is deep within our soul, and the scar cannot heal! For—
my people are an invaded people
my people are a suppressed people—
my people are a suffering people
my people are an oppressed people—
But we are not a defeated people—we are not defeated!

My people are a proud people. Our continuing fight is reflected and embodied in our very culture and history. The incredible endurance and growth of our own unique culture, despite all of the brutal efforts against us, clearly demonstrates that continuing fight. We have never succumbed, we have never melted into your brutal racist society, we have not lost our identity, we have not forgotten our language, we have not given up our very own rich heritage, and we continue to maintain our own communal way of life—

In essence, we have never rejected ourselves!
We are a proud people with
—an intense pride
—a rebellious spirit
—a revolutionary tradition

The maintaining of our own unique and distinctive culture has been our continual rebellion against the white man's invasion.

What Do You Think?

1. What part does the issue of culture play in developing prejudice against an ethnic group?
2. Can minority ethnic groups develop prejudice against the majority? Explain.

9. PORTRAIT OF A KLANSMAN: RAYMOND CRANFORD *

In this article, a Ku Klux Klan Exalted Cyclops is interviewed by Stewart Alsop. To what degree do people like Raymond Cranford influence prejudice and discrimination? Does the Klan spread these

---

* Excerpted from Stewart Alsop, "Portrait of a Klansman: R. Cranford," *The Saturday Evening Post,* April 9, 1966.

*attitudes, or does it merely represent people who already feel that
way? If a person is "born into the Klan," can he escape?*

Raymond Cranford, an Exalted Cyclops of the Ku Klux Klan in
North Carolina, is a bullet-headed man with expressionless, black-rimmed
eyes who wears his hair close cropped, military fashion. Cranford fully
expects to be framed by the Federal Bureau of Investigation, or killed
by Negroes or Communists, and he always has a rifle or pistol within easy
reach. He talks a good deal about the last war, in which he was wounded,
and about the Communists, who are, he believes, getting ready to assume
power, and about guns, which he loves. But wherever a conversation with
Cranford starts, it always comes back to the same subject—what Cranford
calls "niggers."

"The word Negro," he explained, within five minutes of our meeting,
"that's not in my vocabulary. There's colored folks and there's niggers,
there ain't no Negroes."

I first met Raymond Cranford at the airport in Raleigh, N. C., where
we had lunch. That lunch was my first exposure to his way of talking,
which is a kind of brutal monologue. The Raleigh airport restaurant is
desegregated, and I pointed to a Negro who was eating next to a white
man at one end of the lunch counter. I asked Cranford if the Negro's
presence bothered him.

"If that man sitting next him wants to eat like a nigger," said Cranford,
"that's his business. But if that nigger was to come to this table, I'd
know how to handle him. I'd say I'd got some alligators I'd like to
feed." He looked around the table with a small, closed-mouth grin—he
does not show his teeth when he smiles, and he hardly ever laughs. Then
the monologue started. A few excerpts will suggest its flavor.

"A white nigger, that's worse than a nigger. A white nigger's a
man's got a white skin, and a heart that's pumpin' nigger blood through his
veins. If it comes to a fight, the white nigger's gonna get killed before the
nigger."

"You come from Washington? I call Washington Hershey-town—
ninety percent chocolate and ten percent nuts."

"We believe a white man's got his civil rights too. I'll lay down my
life for those rights, if I have to." . . .

"We don't believe in burning crosses on a man's lawn. If I'm
gonna burn a cross, I ram it through the man and burn it." This with
a small grin.

"When the Communists take over, they're gonna kill me quick. Well,
you only got one time to die."

"I got a daughter, she's nineteen years old. I love my daughter,
but I find her with a nigger, I'll take my gun and I'll blow her brains
right out of her head."

These observations are not very pretty or enlightening, and in the time I spent with Raymond Cranford, I heard them repeated almost literally *ad nauseam*. And yet it is worth trying to understand Raymond Cranford, for he is one of a very large number of Americans who are wholly alienated from the comfortable American society that most of us know. In the Klan oath, the world outside the Klan is called "the alien world," and in the eyes of a Klansman like Raymond Cranford, that world is heavily populated by "Communists," "white niggers," and other enemies.

North Carolina has an old and well-earned reputation for moderation in race relations. Nevertheless, as the recent investigation by the House Un-American Activities Committee established, North Carolina's Ku Klux Klan, nonexistent three years ago, is now bigger and better organized than the Klan in any other state. Its membership has been estimated as high as 20,000. The hard core of the Klan is in the flat, sandy, cotton-and-tobacco country in the eastern part of the state, where Negroes make up more than 40 percent of the population. The hard core of this hard core is in Greene County, where Exalted Cyclops Raymond Cranford presides over his klavern.

Cranford was in the Marines in World War II, he told us at lunch, and had been wounded and decorated. "A psychiatrist told me I got backward reflexes," he said. "I got no sense of fear. Till I was twelve years old, I couldn't get to sleep at night without a light in the room. But when I'm in danger, I'm *cool*." . . .

Cranford is deeply proud of being a Klansman. "My daddy and my granddaddy were in the Klan," he says. "I was born in the Klan." He is, he says, "a Klansman full time and a farmer part time." He owns a 200-acre farm with a 22-acre tobacco allotment. In most years his tobacco crop alone brings him a net profit of around $11,000. But Raymond Cranford does not think of himself as a prosperous citizen.

"They wouldn't let a pore white like me past the door of the Waldorf-Astoria in New York," he said, as we walked to the parking lot. "So why should a nigger go anywhere he wants?"

Between the bucket seats of Cranford's red, late-model car there was a bone-handled pistol and cartridge belt, and a rifle hung in a halter arrangement by the left front door. Cranford demonstrated how he would react if a "nigger or Communist" threatened him in the car. When he opened the door, he could fire his rifle without taking it out of its halter. The hollow-pointed bullets, he explained, would catch a man in the legs or stomach. "Mister, with this little gun," he said, "you can blow a hole through a man, you could walk right through it."

"I can outrun any FBI car in the state—I got a supercharged engine," he said, as we started on the drive to Greene County. "Course, the FBI taps my phone. I got an alibi for every cotton-pickin' minute, but they'll find a way to frame me." To the relief of his passengers, he turned out to be a cautious driver, careful about passing, and stopping at all stop signs.

Cranford is very proud of being Exalted Cyclops, or No. 1 man, of his klavern. A klavern is the basic Klan unit, with membership ranging from a dozen or so to a couple of hundred—Cranford said he had about 60 men in his klavern.

He was also, he said proudly, a major in the "V.I.P. Security Guard" of the Klan. As such, he wears a major's oak leaves, and a helmet liner, uniform, and regulation paratroop boots at the Klan's cross-burning rallies. His job is to guard the Grand Dragon, the Imperial Wizard, and other Very Important Persons.

"Fren, you better keep your hands away from your pockets at a rally. You lay a hand on the Grand Dragon or the Imperial Wizard, and fren, you're *daid*." . . .

A man could identify himself as a Klansman if he wanted to Cranford said, but no other Klansman would identify him, on pain of death. "In some places," he explained, "you got white niggers, they'll fire Klan people—they won't say it's because they're in the Klan, but they'll always find some excuse."

Then there are anti-Klan people in Greene County? "Some; but everybody knows they're just after the nigger dollar."

By this time we had arrived at the motel where we were to stay. When Grand Dragon Jones was in the neighborhood some months earlier, Cranford said, the manager refused to give him a room. Cranford gleefully explained how he dealt with this insult to the Grand Dragon.

"I went to the manager, and I said, 'Now, fren, I'm not threatenin' anybody. But I got twenty niggers working at my place, and they're *real* dirty niggers, why I bet they haven't washed for weeks, and they sure *do* stink. Now I want a public apology to the Grand Dragon, and if I don't get it, I'm gonna register those twenty niggers right here. If you take them you'll have to fumigate the place, maybe burn it down. If you don't take them, I'm gonna prosecute you under the Civil Rights Act.' So he apologized."

That evening we drove over to Raymond Cranford's house for supper and found that quite a little party had been laid on for us. . . .

The Cranfords live in a small brick house, close to a village street. The furniture is the kind that is meant to be used, not just looked at. There is an old-fashioned front parlor, a dining room and a "family room" at the back. The party moved into the family room. No liquor was served. Somebody put a record on the phonograph. The song's endlessly repeated refrain was: *Move those niggers north, if they don't like our southern ways, move those niggers north.* Cranford pointed to his young son's school book—there was a big KKK scrawled in ink across its cover. "He's born into the Klan too," Cranford said proudly. . . .

In the living room, after supper, the guns came out. Everybody seemed to have a gun—all the children had toy guns. Cranford showed the shotgun he had won for recruiting members into the Klan, and Littleton passed around his new high-powered rifle. Then Cranford put on his Exalted Cyclops robes, white with a crimson hood. "They call these robes bedsheets," he said indignantly. "Bedsheets! You just feel that satin. That's the finest quality there is."

We got up to go, and I thanked Mrs. Cranford for the delicious chicken dinner. "Now, when you come to write that article," she said, in a sweet-southern voice, "you be fair. You're not fair, I'm coming to Washington with a machine gun." . . .

The next day we went to the town of Ayden, where, Cranford said, "the niggers are stirring up trouble." Outside a store, a line of Negro children were carrying signs reading NO HIRING NO BUYING or WE'RE TIRED OF BEING BAGBOYS AND MAIDS. This trouble, Cranford said, had been "stirred up" by the local head of the N.A.A.C.P., an undertaker called Gratz Norcott.

"He stirs up the trouble, and him being an undertaker, if the trouble gets bad, he stands to get all the business. I tole him, if one of my guys gets hurt, I'm not gonna horse around, I'm comin' after *you*."

Norcott, it turned out, had his office in a small house across the street from the store. Ted Ellsworth suggested that we call on Norcott, and get his side of the story. The idea of a confrontation with Norcott had clearly never occurred to Cranford. But he interpreted the suggestion as a challenge to his courage. So he squared his shoulders and strode into the little house, followed by the Klaliff, the Night Hawk, and us "aliens."

Norcott's office is tiny, and by the time I elbowed my way into it, whatever greetings had been exchanged between Cranford and Norcott had already occurred, and an uncomfortable silence reigned. Norcott, a middle-aged Negro with an expressionless face, was at his desk, with a telephone held against an ear. Occasionally he would mutter something into the telephone, but there were long stretches when he said nothing at all. I shook his hand, and it was wet with sweat, and when he lit a cigarette, the match wavered. But if Norcott was scared by this surprise visit from the Klan, his self-control was remarkable.

For a while, as Norcott held the telephone up to his ear, we white men stood around rather sheepishly—there were only two chairs in the office. Then Norcott held the telephone away from his ear and addressed Cranford in a polite but authoritative tone:

"Mr. Cranford, there are some chairs right across the hall there. Will you fetch a few so these gentlemen can sit down?"

Cranford hesitated a moment, and glared at Norcott, then got the chairs. We all sat down.

At last Norcott put the telephone in its cradle. While he was explaining his side of the "trouble"—the store did most of its business with Negroes, he said, and the Negroes wanted one of the three cashiers' jobs —two young, tough-looking Negroes came into the office, followed by an elderly Negro minister and a Negro doctor. Obviously news of the confrontation had spread rapidly.

The two young men were field workers for Martin Luther King's Southern Christian Leadership Conference. One was a native North Carolinian, the other came from the Bronx. Norcott introduced them, and then introduced Cranford:

"Mr. Cranford here is the Cyclops—is that right, Mr. Cranford? Yes, the *Exalted* Cyclops of the Ku Klux Klan." There was no hint of a smile, only the faint emphasis on the ridiculous adjective.

Cranford, sensing a challenge, glared at the Negro from the Bronx, then addressed Norcott:

"Now, fren, I'm not threatenin' you. I'm just givin' you a bit of advice. You and me, we don't see things the same way, but we'll get along all right, just so long as you don't bring in outsiders to make trouble. If you're gonna bring in outsiders, you could be asking for real *bad* trouble. Now, is that a gamble you want to take?"

"Well, now, Mr. Cranford," said Norcott, his tone polite, almost soothing, "when you had your rallies here last summer, I think I'm right, you brought in Mr. Shelton, the *Imperial* Wizard, I think you call him, from Alabama. And I heard you bring in some *Grand* Dragons, or what is it you call them, from as far away as Ohio. Isn't that right?"

"Well, let me tell you something," said Cranford, "I don't believe in threatenin' a man, or burning crosses to scare him. If I got something I don't like about you, I just walk right up to you in the street and bust you right in the nose."

"Well, now, Mr. Cranford," said Norcott, more soothingly than ever, "I wouldn't walk right up to you and punch *you* in the nose. I'd *discuss* the matter with you. And if we couldn't agree, then I'd put the matter in the hands of the law, because we in the N.A.A.C.P., we believe in the law, we obey the laws of the land."

By this time Cranford was both angry and a little confused, like a bull after the picadors had worked him over.

"I'm against violence," he said, his voice rising, "but I'm going to protect my rights, and if anybody wants a fight, he can get what he wants. Why, few weeks ago, three niggers pulled up beside my car, I seen they had guns, and I put a clip in my gun, and by God . . ."

"SHUT UP, RAYMOND," Pete Young said, suddenly and loudly. Cranford subsided. There was some further sparring. Then Cranford said, rather plaintively, "You nigras talk about discrimination. Why, right here, some cops will give a Klansman a ticket just *because* he's a Klansman."

At this point, Dr. Andrew Best, a Negro physician with a round, good-humored face, intervened for the first time. He spoke with quiet passion;

"But can't you see, that's just what they've been doing to us as long as we've lived, giving us a ticket just because we're Negroes."

"The word 'Negro,' " Cranford said, in a Pavlovian reaction, "that's not in my vocabulary. There's colored folk and there's niggers, there ain't no Negroes."

"Mr. Cranford," said Dr. Best, in a tone of infinite earnestness, "I want to ask you to try to imagine something. I want to ask you to try to imagine what your life would be like if my color was your color and your color was my color. Can you imagine what that would be like?"

"Listen, fren," said Cranford, "do you think life's easy for the pore white man in the South?" Cranford got up suddenly and strode out to his car, followed by the Klaliff and the Night Hawk, while we outsiders shook hands with the Negroes and muttered good-byes. . . .

The Kleagle, the Klokkard, the Night Hawk, Exalted Cyclops Littleton, and their wives and children seemed polite, pleasant-mannered people. Raymond Cranford and the other Klansmen were no doubt brave men and patriots by their own lights. And they were all people who wanted very badly, almost desperately, to be understood. Yet, I never did really understand them.

"Maybe there's something you don't understand, coming from the North," the young Klaliff said. Maybe there is. But how *do* you understand people who seem to be moral people, and who feel quite sincerely that a picture of a woman walking with Negroes, with her shoes off, justifies her murder?

What Do You Think?

1.   What enables the KKK to maintain control in those areas where it is organized?
2.   What factors have caused Raymond Cranford to feel as he does?
3.   Can people like Raymond Cranford ever change?
4.   Can truth be used as a weapon against the type of prejudice and discrimination found in the KKK?

ACTIVITIES FOR INVOLVEMENT

1.   It is often argued, especially by whites, that minority peoples "don't really care,"—that they don't want to improve their status. Review all of

the readings in this chapter for any evidence that you can find that *refutes* this statement. What other evidence could you offer?

2.   The following six items are often given as causes for prejudice or discrimination:

   a. Traditional values or attitudes.
   b. Ignorance.
   c. Scapegoating.
   d. Stereotyping.
   e. Hate.
   f. Fear.

How might each of these lead to prejudice? To discrimination? Rank these items in order of seriousness (from most to least serious) and then compare your ranking with those of your classmates. How would you explain any differences in the rankings? How many of the above entered into the prejudice or discrimination described in the readings in this chapter?

3.   Write a short skit that will illustrate one of the causes of prejudice or discrimination suggested in this chapter. Enact it for your classmates and see if they can discover the point you are trying to make. Then hold a class discussion on how the skit might be improved.

4.   Define a number of the following words and compare your definitions with those of your classmates to see which seem to be stereotypes:

aggression	civil rights	Mexican	Uncle Tom
police	Jew	prejudiced	colored
cop	racism	race	spik
bigot	nigger	tolerance	injun
fuzz	ghetto	brotherly love	honkie
Black Power	integration	whitey	pig

How might the use of stereotyped words cause trouble among police and minorities?

5.   Write or visit two or more of the following human relations agencies to obtain information and materials on prejudice and discrimination:

American Jewish Committee
Anti-Defamation League of B'nai B'rith
American Civil Liberties Union
Catholic Interracial Conference
National Association for the Advancement of Colored People (NAACP)
Student Non-Violent Coordinating Committee (SNCC)
Congress of Racial Equality (CORE)
National Conference of Christians and Jews
National Council of Churches
United Nations
Urban League
American Friends Service Committee

Prepare a classroom or school display of these materials. How are they attempting to reduce prejudice and discrimination? In what ways are their efforts similar? Different? How would you explain these similarities and differences?

6.   Listed below are a number of reasons frequently offered as contributing to the conditions of minorities in the United States today:

a. What passes for education in most schools, from the elementary grades through graduate school, is irrelevant to the needs and concerns of minority students.

b. Police and other law-enforcement officials are more suspicious of members of minority groups, and thus tend to arrest them more frequently.

c. Merchants in minority neighborhoods charge higher prices than are charged elsewhere.

d. Many of the parents of minority children have lost all hope of bettering themselves, and they pass this sense of hopelessness on to their children.

e. Most banks, savings and loans association, and other financial agencies are less willing to assist people from minority groups to "get started" in business for themselves.

f. Many individuals from minority groups are just "naturally" bent on destruction.

g. Many employers are unwilling to place minority individuals in positions of responsibility and authority.

h. Many white individuals are afraid that minority group members will take away much of what they have worked all their lives to attain, and thus they consciously or unconsciously discriminate against minority groups.

What evidence can you offer to support or refute each of these statements? Which, if any, do you think are justified explanations? Hold a class discussion to add other explanations that the class can think of to the list, and then write a short paper (approximately two pages in length) in which you explain why you think any one or two of the reasons offered are or are not justified.

5

Where Does Discrimination Occur?

We have seen that discrimination may be practiced by and directed against individuals or groups within our social structure. What types of organizations exist that have formulated prejudice into a deliberate policy? We have read about the Ku Klux Klan. Within our broader society, do institutions discriminate? What types of people participate in such groups? Are individuals always aware of the discriminatory policies of groups to which they belong? How difficult is the task of eliminating these policies?

1. THE ARTHUR ASHE THING *

Arthur Ashe became the national men's singles tennis champion by defeating the best in the world, including professionals. Can a black national champion play tennis throughout the nation?

The Dallas Country Club has cancelled its annual invitational tennis tournament this year, ending its sponsorship of that attractive event. Reason: Arthur Ashe, the nation's 2nd ranked player, is Negro. "I advised the board that I was going to invite Ashe," says Tournament Director Kenneth Parker, a former ranking player himself. "That did it. They will try to tell you it was for other reasons. Some members had been unhappy with the tournament—it crowded the club for a week with all sorts of strangers—and it would have been turned over to the public Tennis Center's bigger facilities in a year or two anyway; but

---

* "The Arthur Ashe Thing," *Sports Illustrated,* "Scorecard," February 21, 1966; Reprinted by permission. © 1966, Time, Inc.

the Ashe thing definitely brought it to a head. In any country club there are a bunch of old mossbacks, and ours is no different. The club had to do it now, because Ashe is the first Negro but not, obviously, the last.

"Really, the problem was not Ashe but the 50 or 100 Negro followers he would bring. Am I going to stand at the gate and tell them they can't watch Ashe play?"

None of this was printed in the Dallas paper when the event was cancelled.

What Do You Think?

1. What did the tournament director imply when he said, "In any club there are a bunch of old mossbacks, . . ."
2. Could the same thing happen to a Jew? A Russian? Why or why not?

2. HELL'S ANGELS ANGRY OVER SAN FRANCISCO POLICE PRESSURE *

The Hell's Angels are a California motorcycle club that has a reputation for being rough, tough, and outside the law. Can an institution such as a police department discriminate against an individual or a group?

San Francisco police turned "the roust" on the Hells Angels motorcycle club, the Chronicle learned yesterday.

The roust is an old police technique that might be explained loosely as a form of harassment.

Angels are angry about being the target of sudden and constant police pressure, and claim that they are not only the subject of discrimination, but beatings.

One member has lodged a formal complaint with the department's personnel division, and this is now "under investigation." The Angel claims he was arrested without cause on Market Street and taken to the Hall of Justice by four officers of the department's new "tactical unit."

He was told en route, he says, that he was being arrested because he wore the Hells Angels insignia on his jacket and that he was going to be given a little "street justice."

There is a slight disparity between the records at Central Emergency Hospital and the official report on his arrest.

---

* Charles Randebaugh, *San Francisco Chronicle*, December 30, 1967.

The police report says that the man was treated at Central Emergency "for old injury to right eye."

Central Emergency says he was treated for contusion of the right lower lid of the eye due to "a fall."

LEANING

Police do not say, officially, that they are rousting the Angels.

"Roust is a little too heavy as a word," said one high-ranking officer. "Let's say that we're leaning on them."

Whatever the terminology, the Angels say they are being arrested without cause and otherwise harassed. . . .

INCIDENT

One Angel told of an incident in a bar in the Mission where he and four other members had gone for a drink, when suddenly "the place was filled with cops."

He said he and the others were lined up against the wall and searched, then were taken to the station, where the officers "turned us loose out the back door as soon as we had walked in the front door."

"It just doesn't make sense," he added.

Some police believe that Hells Angels may be involved in the Christmas Eve bombing of Park Police Station, where a small, homemade bomb was placed on a window sill.

CALLS

Park Police Station Officer Peter McElligott subsequently received two anonymous phone calls saying the bomb was intended for him because he had arrested several Hells Angels.

"That's not the way we go," a member of the Hells Angels told the Chronicle. "The police are trying to make us the goats."

The Angels have not decided exactly what to do about the roust, but several of the members have suggested compiling a scorecard and then consulting an attorney.

What Do You Think?

1. Are the police prejudiced against the Hells Angels?
2. Could not every criminal claim discrimination in front of the law? Should you be faced with such a claim, how would you respond?

3. A CHARGE OF SEX BIAS IN PHONE SUIT *

Charges of discrimination also appear in the world of business. Might there be a cause-and-effect relation between prejudiced thinking and discrimination in wages?

A suit backed by the Federal Equal Employment Opportunities Commission charged the Pacific Telephone Company here yesterday with discriminating against women employees.

Five female clerks at the company's San Jose office claimed they do the same work as men there—assigning new lines to customers—but get paid $45 a week less.

Pacific Telephone did not comment on the specific charges, but said flatly that "we are not in violation of any Federal or State laws regarding job assignments."

The women charged, in U. S. District Court, that they are paid less because they are classified as plant service clerks, a classification that pays a top of $105.50 a week.

Men doing the same work, they said, are classified as line assigners, a category that pays $149.50 a week.

No women have the higher classification in San Jose, even though the Federal commission said the five women have more experience and training than the men.

After an investigation, the commission asked the telephone company to promote the women to the higher classification. But it said conciliation efforts failed, and thus it backed the suit under the Civil Rights Act of 1964.

What Do You Think?

    1.   Is prejudice involved in this instance in any way?

    2.   Are women in fact discriminated against in the business world? What economic reasons might there be for discrimination?

---

* *San Francisco Chronicle,* May 9, 1968.

4. RALPH RAMIEREZ *

Ralph Ramierez shares a problem with many Mexican-Americans. School institutions seem to have pushed him to the back of the room. Did white attitudes toward Mexican-Americans create Ralph's problem?

Okay, my name is Ralph Ramierez, why should that mean I'm dumb? Yea, I get put in the back seat and told to shut up ever since I was in first grade. Why? I'll tell you why if you'll let. Sure, I don't have the good speech that you do, so most my life I've been told to shut up or been laughed at. Why don't you "Anglos" let us talk—maybe if you'd let us try to tell you how it feels, we could. Sure, we don't use big words and good sentences—how can we, we speaked Spanish for five years till the first grade. Maybe if you only listen you'd be able to feel why I'm angry and mad and—and—all screwed up.

In the first grade I couldn't speak hardly any English. I didn't hardly know what the teacher was saying, and I couldn't answer questions. So what I do? What would you do? I shut up. A lot of us do. Then they gave us those tests! What a laugh—they didn't teach me to read yet.

Then they put us all together and told us we were dumb. Yea, some of them teachers told us right out that we was dumb. Those that didn't, treated us like we were dumb. Well, why didn't you teach us to read and talk before you called us dumb. Sure, all the "Anglos" thought the same thing. And when they grew up they remembered. Ever have a cop yell at you "Hey, Mexican, get out of that car," and then when you started to tell him his question, he say, "shut up Wetback," and phone in to the office to see if you had stolen your own car!

That's why we drop out of school; you never gave us a chance— bad teachers, never did go to a play—they only took the smart Anglos! Never got any new books. Nobody ever let us talk long enough in our bad English to know whether we believed in anything. So finally I turned it all off. Yea, that whole damn thing. Well, I got to sophomore year in college now because a hip girl talked me into going back. They took the time to listen up there—but now, right here today, what are you doing. I feel it; I see it in your faces; I hear it in your voices. You guys trying to put off a poor, dumb Mex! Why don't you help—that's all we want. Help us to read—take a poor, dumb Mex kid to a play. You sure as hell draft him into the army fast.

---

* Taped interview made by Fred Holmes.

What Do You Think?

1.   How important do you think white attitudes were in forcing Ralph Ramierez to drop out of school?
2.   Ralph Ramierez has blamed institutions, specifically schools and the law, for his condition. Do you think he has a case? Explain.

5.   THE HIDDEN FLOWER *

Mr. Kennedy, father of a son who married a Japanese, learns with pain about the injustice of miscegenation laws in this excerpt from a book by Pearl Buck. What effect do such laws have on human dignity?

"Josephine!" he said loudly, "you know that law was made against the niggra!"

"It's the law," she repeated.

He had got up and left her, but before he could sleep he had called his own lawyer, Bancroft Haynes. It was true, the law of the state did forbid Allen's marriage, because the girl had in her the blood of Asia. Now he had to tell the boy somehow.

The door opened and Allen came in with Josui. Mr. Kennedy had dreaded this moment and here it was. He rose slowly to his feet, staring at the girl his son held by the hand, a shy lovely girl, whose cream-white skin was flooding pink and whose great dark eyes were humid with fear. Why, he thought, what a sweet face, what a timid child, a suffering child, anxious to please, pleading to be understood! All his pity, ready and trembling, rushed toward her.

"This is Josui," Allen said.

Mr. Kennedy crossed the room heavily and put out his large soft right hand. "I am glad to see you, ma'am," he said with his finest courtesy. "You have come a long way and I make you welcome." He felt her small firm hand in his and he pressed it gently. "You must be tired and maybe a little homesick."

"Oh, no, thank you," Josui replied in a voice just above a whisper. She was overpowered by Mr. Kennedy's size. So big a man, but instantly

---

she saw how kind. She smiled, her lips quivering and her eyes larger than ever as she looked up at him.

Mr. Kennedy gazed down on her almost tenderly, relieved to see her so obviously not colored. Why, there were plenty of girls in the best Southern families who were darker by a good deal. He would certainly tell Josephine.

"You're a little bit of a thing, aren't you?" he said. He turned to his son. "Are they all as little as she is?"

"Josui isn't so little, Dad," Allen replied. He was heartened. His father had responded at once to Josui's delicate, almost touching charm, and he was proud of her. His father would understand how a man could fall in love with her. His father would be on their side.

Between the two tall men Josui suddenly smiled. She was no longer afraid. This big fat good man who was her father-in-law would help them and everything would be nice. She liked him, she could never be afraid of him, she would be very happy living in his house. It was no wonder that Allen was wonderful, he being the son of such a father. And she also would be a perfect daughter-in-law.

She pulled away from Allen. "Please, Father, sit down," she exclaimed. "Allen, we don't have some tea. Call, please, and tell downstairs to bring up tea and some little eating things."

"I don't want anything to eat," Mr. Kennedy said in the same tender voice. She was such a cute little thing! "I've only just finished my breakfast and Allen will tell you that I'm a hearty eater at breakfast. But then I eat very little in the middle of the day. Night is when I have dinner."

He sat down and she hovered about him. "Some whisky-soda?" she coaxed, "or a coke, maybe?" She had learned to drink and say coke, while they traveled, because she did not like alcohol.

"Well, a whisky-soda, maybe," Mr. Kennedy said to please her.

So Allen must order it and she was not at ease until the boy brought it up on a tray and then she would not let Allen touch the glass or the ice, but she must do everything herself. Only when Mr. Kennedy was served, when she had carried a little table to his side and had set everything exactly upon it and had actually seen him with the glass in his hand, was she at ease. She stood waiting and anxious until he had taken a first sip.

"It is nice?"

"Perfect," he replied heartily, willing to say anything to please her. "Now you sit down, honey, and rest yourself. I want to hear you talk. I want to know how my son is treating you. He better be nice to you!"

"Sit down, Josui," Allen commanded.

She sat down at once, not answering, her graceful little body still unrelaxed, looking from one to the other of the two men.

"Does she spoil you like this all the time?" Mr. Kennedy asked of his son.

"It's the Japanese idea of what a woman ought to do," Allen said, smiling.

"They're wonderful people," his father said.

Then he remembered. Long habit made it easy for him to forget what was sad or hard or troublesome and for the moment he had forgotten. But of course he couldn't talk before this little creature. Her heart would be broken and it must not be. He and Allen must think what to do. He must help his son to do the right thing. But what was the right thing exactly?

He became grave and Josui, reflecting at once the mood of those nearest her, looked at Allen and was afraid again. She wished that he could speak Japanese, for then she could ask him what she had done that was wrong. He did not look at her, and then suddenly she could not bear the silence and the father's almost sorrowful gaze not at her or at Allen but at his glass, the carpet at his feet, the window. She stole across the floor to put her hand on Allen's shoulder. "Do I something wrong?" she inquired in a whisper.

"No, of course not," Allen said in his natural voice, "But I think my father wants to talk to me alone, Josui. Suppose you go in the other room."

She knew instantly that something was very wrong but she obeyed like a child. She walked away to the bedroom door, opened it, went in and closed it noiselessly behind her.

Mr. Kennedy knew then that he had to face it. There was no escape. He put down his glass. "Son, I have bad, bad news."

Allen waited, not answering.

"Had I better give it to you straight?" Mr. Kennedy asked.

"Of course, Dad."

"That's what I thought you'd say."

He leaned forward in his chair and put his elbows on his knees and his big soft hands hung between his knees. He clasped them, his fingers twisted. "Son, your mother is right, I guess. It's not a legal marriage."

"What do you mean?" Allen demanded.

"Not in our state," his father said heavily. "There's an old law, forbidding marriage between the races. Your mother found it somehow. I reckon some of the ladies she goes with heard about it somewhere. Maybe she knew all the time but I don't believe she did."

"That old law was meant for the colored people," Allen said coldly.

"That's right," his father said. He was sweating terribly and big drops burst out of his high forehead and ran down his cheeks by his ears. "But it seems—forgive me son—that it includes everybody not white."

---

1. What control did Mr. Kennedy have over the situation? How did this affect him. How did he feel?
2. Can individuals lose their own identity in a community where prejudice and discrimination are the rule?

6. MEMO FROM A MORMON *

Recently members of the Mormon Church have begun to question the long-standing church policy that prohibits black people from entering the priesthood. Is this institutionalized discrimination?

With the political rise of [former] Governor Romney of Michigan, a Mormon, and the thrust of the Mormon Church into the urban life of our nation, the position of the Negro in the Mormon Church is gaining new attention. There has been a good deal of confusion surrounding this question for some time. Non-Mormons have been confused. As a life-long Mormon, I have been, too.

The Mormon Church taught me that the Negro was not equal to the white in terms of religious rights and opportunities. It taught me that the Negro was cursed with loss of God's priesthood and that the evidence, or mark, of this curse was his dark skin. Consequently, the Negro could not hold the priesthood in the Mormon Church and was thus unequal to the white in a very important sense. But the reasons for this doctrine, and the scriptural evidence behind it, had always seemed unconvincing to me.

Then one evening, I came across an article on the subject that quite surprised me. This article, printed in the *Deseret News,* a Salt Lake City newspaper owned by the Mormon Church, quoted at length one of the highest officials of the Mormon Church, Joseph Fielding Smith, president of the Council of the Twelve Apostles, a body that serves directly under the President of the Church and his two counselors in directing affairs of the Church.

President Smith, whose position has traditionally been the stepping

---

* Excerpted from Jeff Nye, "Memo from a Mormon," *Look,* October 22, 1963. Copyright © 1968 by Cowles Publications, Inc. Reprinted by permission McIntosh and Otis, Inc.

stone to the presidency of the Church, is the Church's doctrinarian. He officially answers the questions of Mormon youth in the Church's monthly magazine, *The Improvement Era.*

The *Deseret News* quoted President Smith as saying:

"The ignorance on the part of writers who do not belong to the Church of Jesus Christ of Latter-day Saints in relation to the views of the 'Mormons' on the status religiously or otherwise of the Negro is inexcusable." . . .

"The Latter-day Saints, so commonly called 'Mormons,' have no animosity toward the Negro. Neither have they described him as belonging to an 'inferior race'."

President Smith went on to quote a passage from the *Book of Mormon* that says Christ "denieth none that come unto him, black and white, bond and free . . ." Next came his major point: "The (Mormon) Church can do more for the Negro than any other church on the face of the earth.

"What other church can baptize them by divine authority and confirm them and give them the gift of the Holy Ghost? What other church can promise them with assurance that they can, if they are faithful and true before the Lord, enter into the celestial kingdom?

"What other church can make a better promise? Moreover we know whereof we speak, for the gospel of Jesus Christ has been restored with all its powers and divine authority.

"The Negro who accepts the doctrines of the Church and is baptized by an authorized minister of the Church of Jesus Christ of Latter-day Saints is entitled to salvation in the celestial kingdom, or the highest heaven spoken of by Paul.

"It is true that the work of the ministry is given to other peoples, and why should the so-called Christian denominations complain? How many Negroes have been placed as ministers over white congregations in the so-called Christian denominations?"

President Smith concluded the article by saying, "It is strange that so many persons are tried and condemned by well-meaning people because of assumed notions and prejudice without a true knowledge of the facts."

This article said just the opposite of what I had learned throughout my teen-age years as a member of the Church.

A few minutes after I had read it, I began to wonder about the knowledge I had acquired as a Mormon.

In the weeks that followed, my inquiries led me to the same answer that I had before reading President Smith's words: The Negro is *not* equal to the white in the Mormon Church, and equality is impossible as long as the Church denies the priesthood to the Negro. This is the policy of the Church.

The Negro is a junior partner in my Church. He is a junior partner because he cannot hold the priesthood, and the priesthood is the foundation of the Church. Only males hold the priesthood, but females share it through marriage. A Negro woman who, according to Mormon doctrine, is also cursed, cannot share the priesthood through marriage.

Today, if a Negro becomes interested in the Church, he can join, and he can be baptized and confirmed as a member by the laying on of hands for the gift of the Holy Ghost. He can come to most of the church meetings. But he cannot pass the sacrament, as the 12- and 13-year-old boys do. He cannot prepare the sacrament, as the 14- and 15-year-olds do. Nor can he bless the sacrament or perform baptisms, as the 16-, 17-, and 18-year-olds do. Nor can he perform any of the other duties of the lesser, or Aaronic, priesthood.

A Negro cannot hold the higher, or Melchizedek, priesthood, or perform any of its numerous and significant functions. He cannot offer the confirmation prayer for a person who has been baptized. He cannot offer the prayer to heal a sick relative or friend or anyone else in the name of the priesthood. Most important, he cannot enter the temple to perform the covenants of the temple. This restricts him from an important blessing, since temple work in the hearts and minds of many Mormons is their choicest earthly blessing.

Deprived of the privileges of the temple, the Negro cannot be married to his wife and sealed to his family *for eternity*. This is the highest covenant that a Mormon may solemnize. It includes various secret and sacred rites and rituals that take place in the temple. Nor can the Negro perform vicarious priesthood ordinances for the dead, which is the other major purpose of the temple. These special, secret rites are a real spiritual blessing to many Mormons. The sanctity and beauty of the temple inject a serene spirituality into the Latter-day Saint. Here, he is renewed and refreshed, ready to face daily life with reinvigorated faith.

Lacking the priesthood, a Negro can never hold any position of leadership in the Church, because the priesthood is the prerequisite for any position of authority. . . .

Can the principle of equality be reconciled with the Mormon doctrine of denial of priesthood? This is the question that troubles me today. Perhaps the new conditions that shape our world today will produce a new view. If we Mormons believe that God is directing our Church, we can hope that God is preparing a new revelation that will revise our present Negro doctrine. If we do not believe this, we can hope that the more liberal element of the Mormon leadership will produce a doctrinal change as the problem intensifies.

What Do You Think?

1. Does the Mormon Church see itself as prejudiced or discriminatory? Explain.
2. Might the Mormon Church's position on black people cause Mormons to question the sincerity of their Church?

7.   INTERRACIAL MARRIAGE AND THE LAW *

In the area of interracial marriage, the individual comes face to face with local institutions of law, church, and community. As recently as 1967, in "Loving vs Virginia," the Supreme Court declared as unconstitutional past marriage laws that discriminated against interracial marriage. Does this in fact end the prejudice and discrimination so closely associated with interracial marriage?

The following excerpt from an article written by Loving's attorney, William D. Zabel, describes in part the historical background of interracial marriage bans.

When a reporter asked former President Harry S. Truman if interracial marriage—miscegenation—would become widespread in the United States, Mr. Truman said, "I hope not; I don't believe in it." Then Mr. Truman asked the reporter that hackneyed question often spouted at anyone advocating racial integration, "Would you want your daughter to marry a Negro?" The reporter responded that he wanted his daughter to marry the man she loved whoever he might be. "Well, she won't love someone who isn't her color," the former President continued, and, as if he had not said enough, added that racial intermarriage ran counter to the teachings of the Bible.

The question of miscegenation can make a man like Truman, whose past support of integration in other respects is not open to question, appear unthinking if not bigoted. The fact of interracial marriage can cause a young Radcliffe-educated "liberal" to refuse to attend the wedding of her only brother, or a civilized, intelligent judge to disown and never again speak to his daughter. How many persons are repelled or at least disconcerted at the mere sight of a Negro-white couple? Perhaps their number tells us how far we are from achieving an integrated society.

If usually tolerant and rational persons can react this way, it is not

---

* Excerpted from William D. Zabel, "Interracial Marriage and the Law," *Atlantic*, October 1965. Reprinted with permission, 1965, The Atlantic Monthly Co.

surprising that many experts consider the fear of miscegenation the strongest reason for the desire of whites to keep the Negro permanently segregated. Next in importance in the "white man's rank order of discrimination," according to Gunnar Myrdal in his classic study, *An American Dilemma,* are other social conventions, the use of public facilities, political franchise, legal equality, and employment. On the other hand, the social and legal barriers to miscegenation rank at the bottom of the Negro's list of grievances; quite naturally, he is more concerned with obtaining a job, decent living accommodations, and an education than with marrying "your daughter." A recent Ford Foundation study of more than seven hundred Negro families in Chicago concluded: "There is no evidence of a desire for miscegenation, or even interest in promoting it, except among a tiny minority. . . ."

The use of laws to ban marriages between persons of different races developed primarily in this country as an outgrowth peculiar to our institution of slavery. Neither the common law of England nor its statutes provide precedents for America's miscegenation laws.

A Maryland statute of 1661 is generally considered the first miscegenation law in America, even though it did not prohibit interracial marriage and was motivated not by a theory of racial superiority, but by economic considerations. Socioeconomic conditions in the colonial period encouraged racial mingling. There was a severe shortage of Negro women in the colonies, and to a lesser extent, of white men of the same social class as the white female indentured servants. These indentured servants and Negro slaves, who often worked together in the fields and lived near each other in similar tenant huts, intermixed and intermarried. By the general custom of the time, a child of such a marriage would be a freeman because he acquired the status of his mother. "And forasmuch as divers freeborn English women . . . do intermarry with negro slaves" by which "a great damage doth befall the master of such negroes," the Maryland statute was passed to stop such marriages by making the female miscegenator a slave for the lifetime of her husband and all children of such marriages "slaves as their fathers were."

According to some historians, after this law was passed, plantation owners encouraged or forced white women, usually indentured servants, to marry Negroes in order to increase the number of slaves. Lord Baltimore, shocked by this practice, had the law changed in 1681 to penalize any master encouraging an interracial marriage and to make such women and their issue free. Masters stopped encouraging these marriages, but they still occurred. And the children of the interracial couples were the financial burden of the masters during their minority because they were the legal children of male slaves. Such children were, however, freed upon reaching maturity. New laws became necessary to compel the servant girls to reimburse the masters for the cost of supporting these children. These laws did not achieve their purpose, and so, finally, all Negro-white marriages were prohibited. . . .

Eventually, miscegenation laws were passed in nearly all the colonies, including Massachusetts in 1705, which also was one of the first states to repeal its law, in 1843. During the nineteenth century, as many as thirty-eight states prohibited interracial marriages. In the period surrounding the Civil War, nine states repealed their statutes. But through the years, Southern states made their laws harsher, Georgia and Virginia going so far as to require all citizens to register and identify their "race" although never establishing a practical means for enforcing the requirement. By 1951, there remained in effect twenty-nine miscegenation statutes. Ten states since 1951 have repealed their statutes. Of these, most were Western states, such as South Dakota (1957), Colorado (1957), Nevada (1959), Nebraska (1963), and Utah (1963), acting at least partially in response to the Negro social revolution . . .

Who is a Negro under such laws? There is no uniform definition, so it is difficult to know. The different definitions create racial chameleons. One can be Negro in Georgia because he had a one-half Negro great-grandmother, and by crossing the border into Florida, become a white because Florida makes him a Negro only if he had a full Negro great-grandmother. The most common definition uses an unscientific percentage-of-blood test usually classifying a Negro as "any person of one-eighth or more Negro blood." . . . Neither the statutes nor science provides a method to determine whether a person is one-eighth Negro or one of the other statutory formulas of fractionalized racial membership. Terms such as "octaroons," "quadroons," and "half-breeds" are misleading except in a fictional or social sense. Genes are not transmitted in predetermined or culturally labeled quantities as the draftsmen of these statutes thought. Detailed genealogies might be used to try to make the statutory racial calculus workable. But even where genealogies are available, they may be unreliable or insufficiently informative on the racial composition of the great-grandparent whose blood allegedly makes the accused a Negro. After all, from one-third to three-fourths of U. S. Negroes have some Caucasian ancestry.

In short, the statutory definitions of Negro are sometimes contradictory, often nonexistent, and usually a combination of legal fiction and genetic nonsense nearly impossible to apply as a practical matter . . .

Today interracial marriage is opposed because of social considerations by the majority of both Negroes and whites. Even those who approve in principle would find it difficult to advise their sons or daughters to enter into such a marriage knowing the unavoidable social problems which confront an interracial couple.

What Do You Think?

1. Are interracial marriages accepted in your community?
2. Will interracial marriages become more acceptable in the future? Explain why you think as you do.
3. What do you find to be the most logical argument for or against mixed marriage?
4. Why do you suppose the scientific, legal, and religious arguments against miscegenation have been accepted for such a long period of time?

ACTIVITIES FOR INVOLVEMENT

1. Fair Employment Practices Commissions are in operation in many states. Does your state have one? If so, write to the commission and ask for an explanation of its procedures. If there isn't one in your state, write your local state assembly representative and ask why not.

2. Select five class members to prepare a panel discussion on the question: "Can an individual discriminate without being prejudiced?" Review the readings included in this chapter to see if any such examples are presented. Then hold a dialogue in which two class members portray Ralph Ramierez and Arthur Ashe discussing the question.

3. Invite a local real estate broker or trade union official to discuss with the class the extent of prejudice or discrimination in housing and labor unions in your area. How do they think such prejudice or discrimination might be reduced? Can it be eliminated?

4. In the 1950's, a major tactic of civil rights workers was the use of nonviolence to break down racial barriers. One tactic frequently employed was for a number of Negro civil rights workers, mostly students, to "sit-in" restaurants and other establishments throughout the South (and elsewhere) and insist on being served. The students, often joined by whites, continued to sit in for many days. As a reminder of their nonviolent purpose, each CORE member would carry a card which read:

Don't strike back or curse if abused;
Don't laugh out;
Don't hold conversations with floor workers;
Don't block entrances to the stores or aisles;
Show yourself courteous and friendly at all times;
Sit straight and always face the counter;
Remember love and nonviolence;
May God Bless you.

In recent years, many observers have felt that such "nonviolence" is being increasingly replaced by more violent means. Watch your local newspapers for two or three weeks to find evidence to support or refute this view. What other evidence exists throughout the country which would support or refute this view? Review each of the statements listed on the CORE card above. How many do you think minority groups would endorse or abide by today? Explain your reasoning.

5.   Many people have been concerned over the spread of "Black Power" and often confused about what it really means. One of the major concerns of many people is whether or not it involves the use of force and violence, and the destruction of property. To what extent is it necessary for a group to use force and violence before it has "power"? If you would argue that some force and violence is necessary, would this imply that those who use "nonviolence" do not have power? Are there different kinds of power?

6.   Write a short story or play in which you try to express the *feelings* of an individual from a minority group in each of the following situations:

  a. Upon being refused service in a restaurant.
  b. Upon being stared at at a party.
  c. Upon being turned down for a job.
  d. Upon being told that a house that you were interested in had just "gone up" rather drastically in price.
  e. Upon having one's children taunted with epithets.
  f. Upon being told that you are "not welcome" in a certain club or organization.
  g. Upon being refused a date by a member of another race.
  h. Upon being told that God is white.

To what extent would you be prepared to argue that an individual would be justified in *feeling* discriminated against in any of the above?

What
Are the Costs?

6

What do we pay for prejudice and discrimination in our society? The cost of burning and looting is obvious, but what of other costs? What of the cost in human emotions, ego destruction, and group anxieties? What of the loss of leadership potential, the individual anxieties produced by feelings of guilt, and the shame involved in destroying another's dignity? What of community fear and the loss of international respect? Can we ever accurately assess such costs?

1. SHOCKING STORY OF APPROVED KILLING IN MISSISSIPPI *

This article about the death of Emmett Till is described as "the real story of that killing." Might it just as accurately be described as an example of the fear, anger, and anxiety toward race that exist in Mississippi?

Disclosed here is the true account of the slaying in Mississippi of a Negro youth named Emmett Till.

Last September, in Sumner, Miss., a petit jury found the youth's admitted abductors not guilty of murder. In November, in Greenwood, a grand jury declined to indict them for kidnapping.

Of the murder trial, the Memphis *Commercial Appeal* said: "Evidence necessary for convicting on a murder charge was lacking." But

---

* Excerpted from William B. Huie, "Shocking Story of Approved Killing in Mississippi," *Look*, January 24, 1956.

with truth absent, hypocrisy and myth have flourished. Now, hypocrisy can be exposed; myth dispelled. Here are the facts.

Carolyn Holloway Bryant is 21, five feet tall, weighs 103 pounds. An Irish girl, with black hair and black eyes, she is a small-farmer's daughter who, at 17, quit high school at Indianola, Miss. to marry a soldier, Roy Bryant, then 20, now 24. The couple have two boys, three and two; and they operate a store at a dusty crossroads called Money: post office, filling station, and three stores clustered around a school and a gin, and set in the vast, lonely cotton patch that is the Mississippi Delta.

Carolyn and Roy Bryant are poor: no car, no TV. They live in the back of the store which Roy's brothers helped set up when he got out of the 82nd Airborne in 1953. They sell "snuff-and-fatback" to Negro field hands on credit: and they earn little because, for one reason, the government has begun giving the Negroes food they formerly bought.

Carolyn and Roy Bryant's social life is visits to their families, to the Baptist church and, whenever they can borrow a car, to a drive-in, with the kids sleeping in the back seat. They call *Shane* the best picture they ever saw.

For extra money, Carolyn tends store when Roy works outside— like truck driving for a brother. And he has many brothers. His mother had two husbands, 11 children. The first five—all boys—were "Milam children"; the next six—three boys, three girls—were "Bryant children."

This is a lusty and devoted clan. They work, fight, vote and play as a family. The "half" in their fraternity is forgotten. For years they have operated a chain of cotton-field stores, as well as trucks and mechanical cotton pickers. In relation to the Negroes, they are somewhat like white traders in portions of Africa today; and they are determined to resist the revolt of colored men against white rule.

On Wednesday evening, August 24, 1955, Roy was in Texas, on a brother's truck. He had carted shrimp from New Orleans to San Antonio, proceeded to Brownsville. Carolyn was alone in the store. But back in the living quarters was her sister-in-law Juanita Milam, 27, with her own two small sons and Carolyn's two. The store was kept open until 9 on week nights, 11 on Saturday.

When her husband was away, Carolyn Bryant never slept in the store, never stayed there alone after dark. Moreover, in the Delta, no white woman or group of white women ever travels country roads after dark unattended by a man. . . .

Juanita Milam had driven from her home in Glendora. She had parked in front of the store and to the left; and under the front seat of this car was Roy Bryant's pistol, a .38 Colt automatic. Carolyn knew it was there. After 9, Juanita's husband, J. W. Milam, would arrive in his pickup to shepherd them to his home for the night.

About 7:30 P.M., eight young Negroes—seven boys and a girl—

in a '46 Ford had stopped outside. They included sons, grandsons and a nephew of Moses (Preacher) Wright, 64, a 'cropper. They were between 13 and 19 years old. Four were natives of the Delta, and others, including the nephew, Emmett [known as Bobo] Till, were visiting from the Chicago area.

Bobo Till was 14 years old; born on July 25, 1941. He was stocky, muscular, weighing about 160, five feet four or five. Preacher later testified: "He looked like a man."

Bobo's party joined a dozen other young Negroes, including two other girls, in front of the store. Byrant had built checkerboards there. Some were playing checkers, others were wrestling and "kiddin' about girls."

Bobo bragged about his white girl. He showed the boys a picture of a white girl in his wallet; and to their jeers of disbelief, he boasted of his success with her.

"You talkin' mighty big, Bo," one youth said. "There's a pretty little white woman in the store. Since you know how to handle white girls, let's see you go in and get a date with her."

"You ain't chicken, are yuh, Bo?" another youth taunted him.

Bobo had to fire or fall back. He entered the store, alone, stopped at the candy case. Carolyn was behind the counter; Bobo in front. He asked for two cents' worth of bubble gum. She handed it to him. He squeezed her hand and said: "How about a date, Baby?"

She jerked away and started for Juanita Milam. At the break between counters, Bobo jumped in front of her, perhaps caught her at the waist, and said: "You needn't be afraid o' me, Baby. I been with white girls before."

At this point, a cousin ran in, grabbed Bobo and began pulling him out of the store. Carolyn now ran, not for Juanita, but out the front, and got the pistol from the Milam car.

Outside, with Bobo being ushered off by his cousins, and with Carolyn getting the gun, Bobo executed the "wolf whistle" which gave the case its name: the wolf-whistle murder. . . .

The Negroes drove away; and Carolyn, shaken, told Juanita. The two women determined to keep the incident from their "men-folks." They didn't tell J. W. Milam when he came to escort them home. . . .

During Friday afternoon, Roy reached the store, and shortly thereafter a Negro told him what "the talk" was, and told him that the "Chicago boy" was "visitin' Preacher." Carolyn then told Roy what had happened.

Once Roy Bryant knew, in his environment, in the opinion of most white people around him, for him to have done nothing would have marked him a coward and a fool.

On Friday night, he couldn't do anything. He and Carolyn were alone, and he had no car. Saturday was collection day, their busy day in the store. About 10:30 Saturday night, J. W. Milam drove by. Roy took him aside.

"I want you to come over early in the morning," he said. "I need a little transportation."

J. W. protested: "Sunday's the only morning I can sleep. Can't we make it around noon?"

Roy then told him.

"I'll be here," he said. "Early."

J. W. drove to another brother's store at Minter City, where he was working. He closed that store at about 12:30 A.M., drove home to Glendora. Juanita was away, visiting her folks at Greenville. J. W. had been thinking. He decided not to go to bed. He pumped the pickup—a half-ton '55 Chevrolet—full of gas and headed for Money. . . .

Big Milam soldiered in the Patton manner. With a ninth-grade education, he was commissioned in battle by the 75th Division. He was an expert platoon leader, expert street fighter, expert in night patrol, expert with the "grease gun," with every device for close-range killing. A German bullet tore clear through his chest; his body bears "multiple shrapnel wounds." Of his medals, he cherishes one: combat infantryman's badge.

Big Milam, like many soldiers, brought home his favorite gun: the .45 Colt automatic pistol. . . .

Big Milam reached Money a few minutes shy of 2 A.M., Sunday, August 28. The Bryants were asleep; the store was dark but for the all-night light. He rapped at the back door, and when Roy came, he said: "Let's go. Let's make that trip now."

Roy dressed, brought a gun: this one was a .45 Colt. Both men were—and remained—cold sober. Big Milam had drunk a beer at Minter City around 9; Roy had had nothing.

There was no moon as they drove to Preacher's house: 2.8 miles east of Money. . . .

Big Milam drove the pickup in under the trees. He was bareheaded, carrying a five-cell flashlight in his left hand, the .45 in his right.

Roy Bryant pounded on the door.

Preacher: "Who's that?"

Bryant: "Mr. Bryant, from Money, Preacher."

Preacher: "All right, sir. Just a minute."

Preacher came out on the screened-in porch.

Bryant: "Preacher, you got a boy from Chicago here?"

Preacher: "Yessir."

Bryant: "I want to talk to him."

Preacher: "Yessir. I'll get him."

Preacher led them to a back bedroom where four youths were sleeping in two beds. In one was Bobo Till and Simeon Wright, Preacher's youngest son. . . .

The visit was not a complete surprise. Preacher testified that he had heard of the "trouble," that he "sho' had" talked to his nephew about it. Bobo himself had been afraid; he had wanted to go home the day after the incident. The Negro girl in the party had urged that he leave. "They'll kill him," she had warned. But Preacher's wife, Elizabeth Wright, had decided that the danger was being magnified; she had urged Bobo to "finish yo' visit."

"I thought they might say something to him, but I didn't think they'd kill a boy," Preacher said.

Big Milam shined the light in Bobo's face, and said: "You the nigger who did the talking?"

"Yeah," Bobo replied.

Milam: "Don't say 'Yeah' to me: I'll blow your head off. Get your clothes on."

Bobo had been sleeping in his shorts. He pulled on a shirt and trousers, then reached for his socks.

"Just the shoes," Milam hurried him.

"I don't wear shoes without socks," Bobo said; and he kept the gun-bearers waiting while he put on his socks, then a pair of canvas shoes with thick crepe soles.

Preacher and his wife tried two arguments in the boy's behalf.

"He ain't got good sense," Preacher begged. "He didn't know what he was doing. Don't take him."

"I'll pay you gentlemen for the damages," Elizabeth Wright said.

"You niggers go back to sleep," Milam replied.

They marched him into the yard, told him to get in the back of the pickup and lie down. He obeyed. They drove toward Money. . . .

Had there been any doubt as to the identity of the "Chicago boy who done the talking," Milam and Bryant would have stopped at the store for Carolyn to identify him. But there had been no denial. So they didn't stop at the store. At Money, they crossed the Tallahatchie River and drove west.

Their intention was to "just whip him . . . and scare some sense into him." And for this chore, Big Milam knew "the scariest place in the Delta." He had come upon it last year hunting wild geese. Over close to Rosedale, the Big River bends around under a bluff. "Brother, she's a 100-foot sheer drop, and she's a 100 feet deep after you hit."

Big Milam's idea was to stand him up there on that bluff, "whip" him with the .45, and then shine the light off down there toward that water and make him think you're gonna knock him in.

"Brother, if that won't scare the Chicago ———, hell won't."

Searching for this bluff, they drove close to 75 miles. Through Shellmound, Schlater, Doddsville, Ruleville, Cleveland, to the intersection south of Rosedale. There they turned south on Mississippi No. 1, toward the entrance to Beulah Lake. They tried several dirt and gravel roads, drove along the levee. Finally, they gave up: in the darkness, Big Milam couldn't find his bluff.

They drove back to Milam's house at Glendora, and by now it was 5 A.M. They had been driving *nearly three hours,* with Milam and Bryant in the cab and Bobo lying in the back.

At some point when the truck slowed down, why hadn't Bobo jumped and run? He wasn't tied; nobody was holding him. A partial answer is that those Chevrolet pickups have a wraparound rear window the size of a windshield. Bryant could watch him. But the real answer is the remarkable part of the story.

Bobo wasn't afraid of them! He was tough as they were. He didn't think they had the guts to kill him.

Milam: "We never were able to scare him. They had just filled him so full of that poison he was hopeless."

Back of Milam's home is a tool house, with two rooms each about 12 feet square. They took him there and began "whipping" him, first Milam, then Bryant smashing him across the head with those .45's. Pistol-whipping: a court-martial offense in the Army . . . but MP's have been known to do it . . . and Milam got information out of German prisoners this way.

But under these blows Bobo never hollered—and he kept making the perfect speeches to insure martyrdom.

Bobo: "You bastards, I'm not afraid of you. I'm as good as you are.
"I've 'had' white women. My grandmother was a white woman."

Milam: "Well, what else could we do? He was hopeless. I'm no bully; I never hurt a nigger in my life. I like niggers—in their place—I know how to work 'em. But I just decided it was time a few people got put on notice. As long as I live and can do anything about it, niggers are gonna stay in their place. Niggers ain't gonna vote where I live. If they did, they'd control the government. They ain't gonna go to school with my kids. And when a nigger even gets close to mentioning sex with a white woman, he's tired o' livin'. I'm likely to kill him. Me and my folks fought for this country, and we've got some rights. I stood there in that shed and listened to that nigger throw that poison at me, and I just made up my mind. 'Chicago boy,' I said, 'I'm tired of 'em sending your kind down here to stir up trouble. Goddam you, I'm going to make an example of you—just so everybody can know how me and my folks stand'."

So big Milam decided to act. He needed a weight. He tried to think where he could get an anvil. Then he remembered a gin which had installed new equipment. He had seen two men lifting a discarded fan, a metal fan three feet high and circular, used in ginning cotton. . . .

Milam: "When we got to that gin, it was daylight, and I was worried for the first time. Somebody might see us and accuse us of stealing the fan."

Bryant and Big Milam stood aside while Bobo loaded the fan. Weight: 74 pounds. The youth still thought they were bluffing.

They drove back to Glendora, then north toward Swan Lake and crossed the "new bridge" over the Tallahatchie. At the east end of this bridge, they turned right, along a dirt road which parallels the river. After about two miles, they crossed the property of L. W. Boyce, passing near his house.

About 1.5 miles southeast of the Boyce home is a lonely spot where Big Milam has hunted squirrels. The river bank is steep. The truck stopped 30 yards from the water.

Big Milam ordered Bobo to pick up the fan.

He staggered under its weight . . . carried it to the river bank. They stood silently . . . just hating one another.

Milam: "Take off your clothes."

Slowly, Bobo sat down, pulled off his shoes, his socks. He stood up, unbuttoned his shirt, dropped his pants, his shorts.

He stood there naked.

It was Sunday morning, a little before 7.

Milam: "You still as good as I am?"

Bobo: "Yeah."

Milam: "You've still 'had' white women?"

Bobo: "Yeah."

That big .45 jumped in Big Milam's hand. The youth turned to catch that big, expanding bullet at his right ear. He dropped.

They barb-wired the gin fan to his neck, rolled him into 20 feet of water.

For three hours that morning, there was a fire in Big Milam's back yard: Bobo's crepe-soled shoes were hard to burn.

Seventy-two hours later—eight miles downstream—boys were fishing. They saw feet sticking out of the water. Bobo.

The majority—by no means *all,* but the *majority*—of the white people in Mississippi 1) either approve Big Milam's action, or else 2) they don't disapprove enough to risk giving their "enemies" the satisfaction of a conviction.

What Do You Think?

1. Why did Roy Bryant react as violently as he did to Emmett Till's actions toward Carolyn Bryant?

2. Why did Moses "Preacher" Wright let Roy Bryant and J. W. Milam take Emmett Till away without a struggle?

3.   What did J. W. Milam mean when he said: "We never were able to scare him. They had just filled him so full of that poison he was hopeless"?

4.   Could Emmett Till have saved himself? Why do you think he acted as he did?

2.   ARSON, LOOTING SPREAD—WATTS BURNS *

Law and order may become unimportant to the victims of discrimination. How can this be explained?

The Negroes are burning the Watts area of L. A. tonight, but no one seems to know just which Negroes are setting the fires or—more important—exactly why.

An angry pall of black smoke is rising from the riot-shattered area like a symbol of torment and tragedy. Only 10 minutes ago, the fire department pulled out—50 pieces of equipment rolled out of flame-gutted 103rd Street and took off.

"They'd rather save their equipment," a fireman said. . . .

POLICE

Some Negroes defend the Police; others say the Police were the cause of it all. But those who live in the immediate burning area know that what is happening here tonight is fundamentally bad for all.

Hardwick says this is not a race riot, that they've been flipping Negroes' cars too. But other Negroes warn that "a Caucasian hasn't got a chance on that street tonight."

A lanky janitor said: "I seen a guy I knew just pack a sawed-off shotgun in his car. Hell, everybody's packing guns tonight. The janitor's name is Lazane Hanzy, and he believes that the trouble stems from two sources: the intolerance and brutality of the police towards Negroes and the lack of jobs for Negroes.

LOVELY

"If City Hall would only better these two things we wouldn't have this, everything would be lovely," Hanzy said. He also had an explanation for the fires—like the big one that burned out Sawaya's Department Store just down the street. "They sell you all this . . . on installments and then they garnishee your wages to get their money." As for the looting, Hanzy said that so many people are broke and without jobs

---

* George Draper, "Arson and Looting Spread," *San Francisco Chronicle,* December 30, 1967.

that they "just figure they'd get in there and get a little something for themselves."

But while the buildings burn and the police march in company strength down the glass-strewn streets, it is hard to concentrate on the basic problem underlying this sprawling riot. Negroes who have lived for years in the immediate area, perhaps buying little cottages while squeezing out a living, blame young thugs from the housing projects that surround Watts.

CRIED

Walter Fuller, a former L. A. policeman and one of the resident Negroes, almost cried as he talked about the riotous scene only 100 yards from his front door. "One thing I hate is a punk—and I've seen a lot of them today," said Fuller. He complained that these punks, setting fire to his own corner of L. A., come from the housing projects and are not part of the local community of Negroes.

As Fuller spoke a hand-thrown fire bomb hit another store, and smoke bellied from its shattered window.

"You see," he said helplessly, "there go more jobs for Negroes."

A truck driver named Charlie stood on the corner of 103rd and Coryston, watching the fire trucks pull out. Across the street was a looted liquor store, a smashed department store with four private Negro guards defending it, and a vacant store with a faded sign: "Roosevelt for Mayor." Charlie says the reason for the riots is that "everyone has been evading and ignoring." The police, he explained, have failed to take action against "some people everyone knows should have been put away," but at the same time they have indiscriminately arrested Negroes without sorting out the good from the bad. . . .

The Watts area is plagued with ignorance, unemployment, hopelessness, and frustration. The people here are Deep South Negroes who moved West; and, in an ironic sense, Los Angeles is harvesting the fruit of the Deep South. . . .

COMMUNICATION

Another cause of this disastrous social explosion was suggested by Bob Kelly, the Negro Accountant for Fremont High School. The school here in Watts has a student population of between 3,000 and 4,000— 95 per cent Negro; the teachers, Kelly said, are 65 per cent to 75 per cent Negro.

"The trouble here as I see it," Kelly said, "is the communications between the Negro community and City Hall have broken down." The people from this area, he explained, do not receive a hearing from City Hall when they go there to discuss their problems. "You might as well forget it."

The Watts area rioters, according to Kelly, are school drop-outs, unemployed and qualified only for unskilled work, of which there is very little—the type of people that have no respect for Dick Gregory or Martin Luther King.

As Kelly talked, smoke suddenly billowed upward from the Safeway Store a block away. "I'll be in the window of my house tonight," Kelly said. "I'll guarantee you if someone throws a fire bomb at my house he'll be laying out there in the morning."

What Do You Think?

1. Why would black rioters burn down black-owned stores?
2. Why do citizens of Watts offer so many different explanations for the rioting?
3. If the majority in Watts felt law and order desirable, why did they let rioting develop?

3.   FREE AT LAST *

How much leadership potential has been destroyed on reservations and in slums? How much will be destroyed by the gun?

My personal trials have taught me the value of unmerited suffering. If only to save myself from bitterness, I have attempted to see my personal ordeals as an opportunity to transfigure myself and heal the people involved in the tragic situation which now obtains. I have lived these last few years with the conviction that unearned suffering is redemptive.

Martin Luther King
from "Strength to Love"

He was a short man, only 5′ 6″, and his powerful head and neck were set atop an almost fragile body. He was kind to his friends, and unceasingly loyal, but essentially withdrawn, intense, even humorless.

His cause came before everything; he would not be dissuaded from its pursuit; he never relaxed. Perhaps that was why, when he died, many were surprised to learn that he was only 39.

PURE DETERMINATION

Born the son of a Baptist minister in Atlanta, Ga., he influenced the decade and the century in which he lived probably as much as any man,

---

* Excerpted from "Free at Last," *This World,* April 14, 1968.

and he did it without ever holding any office higher than that of pastor of the Ebenezer Baptist Church of Atlanta. He held sway with the sheer purity of his determination and the clarity of his will. It was not his words which inspired so much as himself—his presence, his existence, his survival.

He had been jailed, beaten, kicked, shot at, threatened, stabbed, vilified, yet his message was always the same: Love everyone; moral force is stronger than physical force; we shall overcome. He was, as someone once said, Mahatma Gandhi in a business suit.

He had come to Memphis to lend his voice and his presence to a strike by that city's garbage workers, 98 per cent of them Negro. More, he had come to Memphis to prove that he was still the leader of his people, that non-violence was still their way. His first Memphis march had ended in disaster—burning, looting, rioting—and he had returned to lead another march, this one (he hoped) peaceful.

ON THE BALCONY

On Thursday, April 4, he had returned to his room at the Lorraine Motel on Mulberry street, four blocks south of Beale street, to wash up and change before dinner. Just before 6 P.M., he had walked out on the second-floor balcony alone, perhaps to think, and stood at the railing, looking out over the small parking lot.

A group of friends inside the room, and another in the courtyard below, heard him call out to his oldest friend and closest associate, the Rev. Ralph Abernathy, "I'll be right with you." Then a single shot echoed off the bare concrete.

As his friends ran toward him, he crumpled soundlessly to the floor, bleeding from a gaping three-inch hole in his neck. One observer said that his lips formed a final syllable: "Oh." The Rev. Abernathy found a towel and used it to stop the bleeding and cover the wound, but it was already too late. The spinal cord of the Rev. Dr. Martin Luther King, Jr. had been severed. He was dead.

I have a dream . . . I have a dream that my four little children will one day live in a nation where they will not be judged by the color of their skin but by the content of their character.

Martin Luther King,
at the March on Washington, 1963

What Do You Think?

1. What did Martin Luther King have that made him a leader?
2. What did the black man lose when Martin Luther King was assassinated? What did we all lose?

4.   REAL POVERTY—PLIGHT OF THE AMERICAN INDIAN *

Indians in the United States have long been the object of prejudice and discrimination. Less than ninety years ago they were hunted in California like rabbits—for sport. How has the Indian fared in the modern era?

Window Rock, Arizona

If Indians themselves take the promise of better days ahead with a large grain of salt, the reason is not far to seek. They have been promised better things ever since the white man began to move westward two centuries ago.

Today, abject poverty is a way of life for the average Indian. Yet the antipoverty dollars and workers that abound in big-city slums are just beginning to move to Indian reservations.

So-called *de facto* segregation existed in Indian schools long before civil-rights advocates coined the phrase. It still is the rule, not the exception. Yet, there's no busing of large numbers of white children to integrate Indian classrooms.

And medical care? On Southwestern reservations, thousands of Indians are blind, or going blind, from trachoma, an eye disease. But Government health services for Indians have been spread too thin for control of the disease.

A LOOK AT ONE TRIBE

Typical of the plight of many tribes today is that of the Navajos. Their reservation is located in the northeastern corner of Arizona, with some land extending eastward into New Mexico and northward into Utah.

The Navajo reservation is a vast and desolate land—15 million acres of desert, semi-arid plains, and mountains. Here live more than one fourth of all Indians on reservations today. Life for them contrasts sharply with that in the affluent society of the white man in such cities as Phoenix, Albuquerque and Denver, each only a few hours' drive away.

Living within the vastness of Navajoland is a population somewhere between 106,000 and 120,000. An exact count is not possible because many families in remote areas have children without reporting them. A total of 380,000 Indians are on U. S. reservations.

---

* Excerpted from "Where the Real Poverty Is—Plight of the American Indian," *U. S. News & World Report,* April 25, 1966. Copyright © 1966 U. S. News & World Report, Inc.

When the Navajos roamed the Southwest at will, they were a proud and self-sufficient tribe. Their freedom ended with "The Long Walk" in 1865. That year, Col. Kit Carson and his troopers climaxed a ruthless, scorched-earth campaign against the Navajos by rounding up 9,000 of their men, women, and children. This band was marched 300 miles to Fort Sumner, in New Mexico. The Navajos spent three years in exile. In 1868, the U. S. Government signed a treaty with the Navajos and returned them to a reservation in their homeland. Over the years, the reservation has been expanded to its present 15 million acres.

DINEH AND THE ANGLOS

The Navajos still are a proud people. They call themselves *Dineh,* which means "the people." Americans are called "Anglos." Navajos consider themselves superior to other Indians and other races. But tribal leaders at Window Rock, capital of the reservation, grapple with problems as monumental as those in many an underdeveloped country.

Poverty is widespread. While an income of below $3,000 a year may mean poverty in the "Great Society" of the white man, a Navajo family with that kind of money is well-to-do in the eyes of other Navajos.

Illiteracy is the rule rather than the exception. Under the 1868 treaty, the U. S. Government is supposed to give Navajo children a free education. Even so, 7 out of 10 adults are unable to read or write the English language.

Unemployment is so high on the reservation as to make so-called pockets of poverty in other parts of the U. S. look prosperous. Raymond Nakai, tribal chairman, estimates that 19,000 are jobless out of a total work force of 30,000.

Housing is substandard by any measure. Most Navajo families live in hogans—small, circular huts of log and adobe without running water or electricity. Others live in frame houses that, if anything, are less adequate than the hogans.

Infant mortality is high. It averages out at 40.3 deaths per thousand births in the first year of life. That compares to a U. S. average of 25.3. Yet, despite high infant mortality, Navajo leaders face a population explosion. Numbers are increasing at the rate of about 3 to 4 per cent a year. The U. S. average is 1.5 per cent.

The Federal Government has been spending more than 50 million dollars a year to improve the Navajos' lot. Most of this, 36.7 million this year, is spent by the Bureau of Indian Affairs, known simply as the BIA. The rest is spent by the U. S. Public Health Service.

KILL AND CURE

Says a BIA official: "People often ask: 'You've been running Indian affairs for 150 years. Why haven't you made more progress?' They forget that for the first 100 of these years we were busy killing off Indians, rounding them up, and pushing them as far out of the way as possible onto reservations in isolated areas. Only in the last generation have we made any real effort to bring the Indians into modern life."

BIA's major effort on the reservation is education. There are 48 boarding schools on the reservation. Nearly half the Navajo children must attend these because distances are too great to bus them to and from their homes. Other children go to BIA day schools and to mission schools. A few attend public schools with white children. School attendance has improved markedly in recent years. In the 1951–52 school year, only 13,135 were in class out of a school-age population of 26,336. In the 1964–65 school year, the comparable figures were 40,256 out of 45,969. Still, that leaves nearly 6,000 children outside classrooms.

Large numbers of children arrive at school age speaking only Navajo. To help them overcome this handicap, the Bureau has pre-school classes in which 6-year-olds get a year of training in the English language. Despite all the money spent on schools, many Navajo leaders feel that the educational effort misses the mark.

A NAVAJO'S STORY

One of these is Peter McDonald, a Navajo who left the reservation to get a college education and a good job, but has returned to try to help his people. The trouble with BIA schooling, as Mr. McDonald sees it, is that the Indian children are taught "to be like a white man, and think like a white man." The result, says Mr. McDonald: "They completely lose their self-identity as Navajos. They can't live within their own culture and they can't live in the affluent society of the white man. So you get mixed-up kids, and they give up. This is happening to many of our young people between the ages of 16 and 30." . . .

Some of the younger generation are getting away to college. There is a scholarship fund derived from interest on 10 million dollars on deposit in the U. S. Treasury. In the 1964–65 academic year, 536 Navajos entered college. Of these, 122 dropped out. In the current year, 596 are in college.

THE RELOCATION PROGRAM

As with other Indian tribes, there have been attempts to move Navajos off the reservation into the mainstream of U. S. life. Under the "direct employment-assistance program" started in 1952, a total of 6,500 Navajo men and women have been relocated in such areas as San Francisco, Los Angeles, Denver, Dallas, Chicago, and Cleveland. The Government pays transportation and initial living expenses and helps the Navajo find a home and a job. A BIA official estimates that about one third have returned to the reservation.

Mr. McDonald, however, puts the figure closer to 50 per cent and says: "One reason for this failure is that people from the reservation haven't learned to live with people outside. As a result, many have tagged relocation as not the right thing to do. Now others don't want to leave because they feel the program is unsuccessful." But basically, says Mr. McDonald, most Navajos feel that "the reservation is their home and they want to make a go of this place."

What Do You Think?

1. What effect has poverty had upon the way an Indian might look at the United States?

2. What does Mr. McDonald mean when he says, "One reason for this failure [to get along off the reservation] is that people from the reservation haven't learned to live with people outside"?

3. Are there any parallels between Indian life and the life of the black man in the ghetto? Differences? Might some of the solutions mentioned apply to both groups?

5. EMOTIONAL WEARINESS *

Experiments with animals have shown that insecurity and fear can cause them to commit suicide. What effect has insecurity and fear had upon minorities in the United States?

A harried young mother, having exhausted the resources of several social agencies, turned to the psychiatrist as a last resort.

She told of her difficulties by describing various crises. The younger children were sick and two older boys had disappeared the previous evening. A riot had broken out on that same evening and she feared for the safety of her sons.

She lived with her five children in a rat-infested apartment. She had never been married and most of her twenty-six years had been spent in public housing projects, living on welfare grants. With five children, she ran out of money near the middle of the month. Then her mother, who could scarcely afford it, would help her buy food. If the groceries were paid for, her roof would begin leaking, and once again she would call the housing office, only to be insulted.

---

* Excerpted from William H. Grier and Price M. Cobbs, *Black Rage.* New York, N. Y.: Basic Books, Inc., 1968.

The most bitter outburst was reserved for the Welfare Department. It was headed by a "boss man" who, she believed, found delight in harassing black women. No one had any privacy. The woman next door awakened in the middle of the night, trembling with fright, to discover that the noise at the window was a social worker peering in to determine if a man was sleeping there.

The patient despised public charity, but having stopped school after the ninth grade, she found her meager skills of little use. Some of her neighbors worked as domestics, but only those with few or no children. If a woman had more than two young children, she could not earn enough to pay a sitter. On and on she went. Through most of her narrative she maintained her composure. But as she was relating an incident of little consequence, the tears came and, as she wept, her strength was revealed.

If the resources and imperfections of this young woman were unique to her, her story would not assume such importance. Familiar concepts could adequately describe her intrapsychic conflict. We would search her past for early trauma, distorted relationships, and infantile conflicts. The social milieu from which she came would be considered but would not be given much weight. Our youthful subject, however, is black and this one fact transcends all others.

She perceives herself and her surroundings in a manner deeply influenced by this fact. The dismal quality of her life shows how little society thinks of her. Six generations have passed since slavery, and her view of life's possibilities is the same as that of a slave on a Georgia plantation. The reluctant conclusion is that her assets and liabilities are the same as that slave's. She is wily, resourceful, and practiced in the art of survival. But, like her "soul sister" in bondage, she is a victim from the time of her birth. This society has placed her at a disadvantage from which she cannot recover. However visible her deficiencies, the true burdens are subtle and strike at her soul. For the more we become immersed in her problems, the more her life spells out a tragedy.

She meets her problems with ordinary defenses. But *her* difficulties have existed for hundreds of years. The pathology she shows is common to most Negroes. The curbing of her aggression began at an early age. It was in large measure determined by a society that is frightened of her. Beneath her passivity lies anger which might otherwise be directed at white people. As a consequence, we see the dependency about which so much has been written. This is another legacy of slavery. In the morning of her life, she saw her mother and other black adults vulnerable to the whim of white persons. From this it would seem logical that she could become as helpless in this society as her enslaved ancestors. To be prevented from growing and maturing is to be kept in a state of dependency.

The means by which she controls her anger have a direct link to the silent war between master and slave. She must be cautious. This may be why she speaks of the "boss man" with such bitterness. She sees him as free to hurt her, while she can never act on her hate for him. That they are both trapped in such an unequal contest is again a tribute to the unchanging nature of America.

In meeting the world, she seems defensive, as if protecting herself from a thousand slights. Her armor, however, guards against real danger. The suspiciousness may seem excessive, but to relax can be to invite disaster. If these types of character traits are seldom encountered in whites, it is because they do not face the same assaults or grow up in the same climate of hatred. As a result, this woman exhibits emotional weariness. The reality of being alternately attacked, ignored, then singled out for some cruel and undeserved punishment must extract its toll. That penalty may be a premature aging and an early death in some black people. To be regarded always as subhuman is a stultifying experience.

What Do You Think?

1. Is there anything other than a dollar and cents cost apparent in this incident?
2. What kinds of behavior might develop from the psychological condition described?

6. A MILLSTONE ROUND OUR NECK *

Have you ever wondered if people in other lands were aware of our problems and, if so, what they thought?

Trains running through the sub-continent of India are as slow, as crowded, and as uncomfortable as one might suspect. Their only positive quality is a product of these factors—people must sit very close to other people for long periods of time. It is like being in a crowded elevator for six hours. In these conditions you are forced to communicate with your fellow man.

Indians love to talk of India. They will defend their arranged marriage system by the hour. They will talk of population and food problems, international affairs, almost anything except their caste system. In attempting to penetrate this closely guarded area a strange phenomenon

---

* By Fred R. Holmes.

emerges. With Americans the Indian has developed a sure-fire method for changing the subject—he attacks white American injustice to the black man. Our racial problems are front-page news in India; therefore it is not only the university-educated Indian who is aware of our problems. It seems almost a fetish with the less-educated to ask about our race problem and then shake their heads in an understanding though disapproving fashion. A druggist from Bombay put it this way, "Why do Americans continue to exploit the Negro; you have enough wealth to go around." This type of statement is one that most Americans would not let pass, but would try to explain. The Indian is thus off the hook about his caste problem.

In an attempt to probe the caste issue an American interrupted a young Indian government employee. The employee's reaction was immediate and devastating, "Please wait until I finish. Don't treat me as if I were one of your American Negroes!"

Our treatment of minorities is thrown at us even when discussing international affairs. "How can you sell a policy of democracy and free will in Southeast Asia when you don't practice democracy at home?" The college math professor responsible for the above observation left a bumpy two-hour train session with this parting shot: "You Americans would do much better in Asia if you talked less about dignity and democracy and more about productivity and efficiency."

What Do You Think?

    1.   What might our minority problem cost us in dealing with other nations?

    2.   Indians are aware of our minority problems. Are you aware of any other nations' minority problems?

ACTIVITIES FOR INVOLVEMENT

    1.   A person's image of himself depends in part on how he sees himself with regard to others around him. Listed below are a number of factors which various people have suggested are influential in the development of a strong self-image:

    a. Bodily development and physique.

    b. Looks.

    c. Material success.

    d. Money.

    e. Pride in one's heritage and traditions.

    f. Emotional support from friends and family.

To what extent do you think that each of these factors are important in the development of a self-image of worth? Add any additional factors that you think are important, and then rank the amended list in order of importance (from most to least important). How can the self-image of all people be enhanced? Are there any ways that are especially effective for minority peoples?

2.　　Review all of the articles included in this chapter and then prepare a list of the costs, both observable and hidden, of prejudice and discrimination. Compare your list with other members of the class and then try to develop a master list. Ask your school newspaper to run a series of articles on each of the costs which the class feels are most costly.

3.　　Many radical groups today view the costs of prejudice and discrimination in terms of the dehumanization of individuals rather than the loss of dollars. They argue that this cost is so great that the destruction of the established system is the only workable solution. How would you respond to such an argument? Write a "letter to the editor" in which you explain your response. How might those who argue for the destruction of the system reply?

4.　　Develop your own tutorial or "head start" program in your community. With some classmates, visit a number of nearby elementary schools and offer your services as tutors or assistants for so much time per week. Perhaps your school can sponsor a number of elementary schools and establish a tutorial program for the community.

5.　　Consult the school librarian to obtain sources so that you might determine the validity of the following statements about the status of minority individuals in the United States today:

　　a. If you are a member of a minority group, your income on the average will be 20 per cent below that of a comparable individual who is white.
　　b. If you live in a slum or ghetto area, your chance of having a crime committed against your person or property is at least ten times greater than if you live in suburbia.
　　c. If you are nonwhite, the odds are twice as great that you will be unemployed than if you are white.
　　d. More money per pupil is spent in schools on white children in large cities (over 250,000 population) than on black children.
　　e. If you are nonwhite, your median family income will be at least $1500 per year less than if you are white.
　　f. If you are a white college graduate, your lifetime earnings will be half again as much as they will be if you are nonwhite.

How many are completely accurate? Do further research to obtain additional examples of the differences existing among various groups in the United States.

7

What Are the Solutions?

As a nation we have only recently accepted the idea that prejudice and discrimination are major problems. Solutions have been proposed, both simple and complex. Different groups within minorities themselves disagree on how to solve the problems. Can integration ever be accomplished for the black man and the Indian? How do Mexican-Americans ever break away from the stereotypes with which they have been tagged? Will hard work and a good job end prejudice and discrimination? Are there solutions to these problems?

1. "GASOLINE FIRE BOMBS CAN BE USED EXTENSIVELY" *

A militant underground organization called RAM suggests the following:

". . . huddle as close to the enemy as possible so as to neutralize his modern and fierce weapons . . . (diminishing) central power to the level of a helpless, sprawling octopus. By day sporadic rioting takes place and massive sniping. Night brings all-out warfare, organized fighting and unlimited terror against the oppressor and his forces . . ."

Instructions to a guerrilla force operating in the jungles of Southeast Asia? Hardly! This is advice offered by Rob Williams, the chief theoretician and organizer of a black militant underground group called the Revolutionary

---

* Excerpted from Russell Sackett, "Plotting a War on Whitey," *Life,* June 10, 1966.

Action Movement or RAM. They see a point in the near future in which Black hate and white racism will force a solution.

"The weapons of defense employed by Afro-American freedom fighters must consist of a poor man's arsenal. Gasoline fire bombs can be used extensively. During the night hours such weapons thrown from rooftops will make the streets impossible for racist cops to patrol . . . gas tanks on public vehicles can be choked up with sand . . . long nails driven through boards and tacks with large heads are effective to slow the movement of traffic on congested roads at night. Derailing of trains causes panic. Explosive booby traps on police telephone boxes can be employed. High powered sniper rifles are readily available. Armor piercing bullets will penetrate oil storage tanks from a distance. Flame throwers can be manufactured at home."

What Do You Think?

1. Would you support this proposal? Why or why not?
2. What might be the final result if such attitudes spread?

2. WHAT WE WANT. WHAT WE BELIEVE *

While RAM calls for violence on the East Coast, the Black Panthers in California call for a general mobilization of black people to carry out their program. Can militant programs force an end to prejudice and discrimination?

1. We want freedom. We want power to determine the destiny of our black community. We believe that black people will not be free until we are able to determine our destiny.

2. We want full employment for our people. We believe that the federal government is responsible and obligated to give every man employment or a guaranteed income. We believe that if the white American businessmen will not give full employment, then the means of production should be taken from the businessmen and placed in the community so that the people of the community can organize and employ all of its people and give a high standard of living.

---

* "October 1966 Black Panther Party Platform and Program," *The Black Panther,* October 19, 1968.

3. We want an end to the robbery by the white man of our Black Community. We believe that this racist government has robbed us and now we are demanding the overdue debt of forty acres and two mules. Forty acres and two mules was promised 100 years ago as restitution for slave labor and mass murder of black people. We will accept the payment in currency which will be distributed to our many communities. The Germans are now aiding the Jews in Israel for the genocide of the Jewish people. The Germans murdered six million Jews. The American racist has taken part in the slaughter of over fifty million black people; therefore, we feel that this is a modest demand that we make.

4. We want decent housing, fit for shelter of human beings. We believe that if the white landlords will not give decent housing to our black community, then the housing and the land should be made into cooperatives so that our community, with government aid, can build and make decent housing for its people.

5. We want education for our people that exposes the true nature of this decadent American society. We want education that teaches us our true history and our role in the present-day society. We believe in an educational system that will give to our people a knowledge of self. If a man does not have knowledge of himself and his position in society and the world, then he has little chance to relate to anything else.

6. We want all black men to be exempt from military service. We believe that black people should not be forced to fight in the military service to defend a racist government that does not protect us. We will not fight and kill other people of color in the world who, like black people, are being victimized by the white racist government of America. We will protect ourselves from the force and violence of the racist police and the racist military, by whatever means necessary.

7. We want an immediate end to POLICE BRUTALITY and MURDER of black people. We believe we can end police brutality in our black community by organizing black self-defense groups that are dedicated to defending our black community from racist police oppression and brutality. The Second Amendment to the Constitution of the United States gives a right to bear arms. We therefore believe that all black people should arm themselves for self defense.

8. We want freedom for all black men held in federal, state, county, and city prisons and jails. We believe that all black

people should be released from the many jails and prisons because they have not received a fair and impartial trial.

9. We want all black people when brought to trial to be tried in court by a jury of their peer group or people from their black communities, as defined by the Constitution of the United States. We believe that the courts should follow the United States Constitution so that black people will receive fair trials. The 14th Amendment of the U. S. Constitution gives a man a right to be tried by his peer group. A peer is a person from a similar economic, social, religious, geographical, environmental, historical, and racial background. To do this the court will be forced to select a jury from the black community from which the black defendant came. We have been, and are being tried by all-white juries that have no understanding of the "average reasoning man" of the black community.

10. We want land, bread, housing, education, clothing, justice, and peace. And as our major political objective, a United Nations supervised plebiscite to be held throughout the black colony in which only black colonial subjects will be allowed to participate, for the purpose of determining the will of black people as to their national destiny.

When, in the course of human events, it becomes necessary for one people to dissolve the political bands which have connected them with another, and to assume, among the powers of the earth, the separate and equal station to which the laws of nature and nature's God entitle them, a decent respect to the opinions of mankind requires that they should declare the causes which impel them to the separation.

We hold these truths to be self-evident, that all men are created equal; that they are endowed by their Creator with certain unalienable rights; that among these are life, liberty, and the pursuit of happiness. That, to secure these rights, governments are instituted among men, deriving their just powers from the consent of the governed; that, whenever any form of government, becomes destructive of these ends, it is the right of the people to alter or to abolish it, and to institute a new government, laying its foundation on such principles, and organizing its powers in such form, as to them shall seem most likely to effect their safety and happiness. Prudence, indeed, will dictate that governments long established should not be changed for light and transient causes; and, accordingly, all experience hath shown, that mankind are more disposed to suffer, while evils are sufferable, than to right themselves by abolishing the forms to which they are accustomed.

But, when a long train of abuses and usurpations, pursuing invariably the same object, evinces a design to reduce them under absolute despotism, it is their right, it is their duty, to throw off such government, and to provide new guards for their future security.

What Do You Think?

1. How do you feel about what the Panthers "believe"? Is it consistent with what they "want"?
2. What historical document do the Panthers quote above? What do they wish this document to do for their program?
3. Can black militancy change prejudice or does it just alter discrimination?

3.   BIRMINGHAM—KEEPING OUR FINGERS CROSSED *

As spectacular as the militant groups are, they represent only a very small proportion of those concerned with the problems of prejudice and discrimination. Since 1954 the Courts and Congress have attempted to alter discrimination through law. Can law be effective in altering human attitudes?

Perhaps it is only Birmingham purging itself. This city, whose violence and murder spawned the Civil Rights Bill last summer, is now the hopeful symbol of Southern compliance with the new Act. Compliance in moderate, progressive Atlanta would have been no surprise. In segregationist, tension-ridden Birmingham, it seems a miracle. . . .

One motel (which will remain nameless) was schizophrenic about the new law's public accommodations section. When other motels and hotels decided to admit Negroes the moment President Johnson signed the new law, it threatened to hold out. City officials pleaded with the managers:

"The choice of course is yours, but if you can't go along please resign from the motel association. It is vital when the association issues its announcement of compliance that it be unanimous."

Reluctantly, the holdout went along.

One place to view the new Birmingham is the Parliament House, a swank motel with plush lounges and elegant bars—and, of course, a lily-white clientele until now. At the Parliament House one day last

---

* "Birmingham—'Keeping Our Fingers Crossed'," *The New Republic,* August 8, 1964.

week, two Negro young women chatted softly over their meal in the pleasant sun-lit lunchroom, surrounded by whites.

In the heart of downtown Birmingham, Abe Slotnik's 20th Century Restaurant, where lawyers and bankers like to eat lunch, was all white on the day we stopped in. "No one's come in here," Slotnik said. "When they do, they'll be served just like you. I'm not fighting the government."

What has happened in Birmingham the past few weeks is not the start of the biracial millenium. But as a case study of compliance with a law repellent to the majority, today's Birmingham story is as encouraging as last year's violence was frightening.

It starts with a document composed by Billy Hamilton, the executive secretary of Mayor Albert Boutwell, at the instruction of the Mayor and the request of the Chamber of Commerce. The document has three features:

First, it makes no effort to "sell" compliance to reluctant businessmen.

Second, it states briefly that "the real danger of disorder or disruption of business will lie in reaching no decision at all, in making no plans" to deal with the sweeping changes of the new law. The absence of plan, it adds, "will leave revolutionary elements free to operate on their own initiative—in effect, 'fill a vacuum.' "

Third, it pledges police protection to proprietors of restaurants, hotels, motels, lunch counters and other "public accommodations," whether they plan to comply with the law or resist it until tested in the courts.

This pledge of police protection by the city of Birmingham, working with the business community, was the foundation on which the city built its compliance program. The dynamics of the civil rights revolution, particularly in the South, have proved that a reliable police force under the direction of men committed to law enforcement is the big obstacle to rule of the mob. . . .

There is a great lesson in Birmingham. Over the years, public figures from Dwight Eisenhower to Barry Goldwater have said that progress in civil rights depends on a change in men's hearts, not new laws. Birmingham today seems to prove otherwise, that new laws are what make progress possible.

What Do You Think?

1. Why do you think the law was effective in Birmingham?
2. Will the law in fact change the behavior patterns of men?

4. ANT HILL *

The Mexican-American wants equal opportunity in the job market and in education. He also wants status. Is it possible to maintain a separate culture and yet have equal opportunity?

Displaced by automation or victims of racism, there exists the reality of poverty—economic poverty—which is the chicanos' reality. This is understood by every chicano, to deny it is cruel and reproachable. Awareness of our inferior position means that we are aware of the superior, of those who keep us down from above. The chicano can now decide what he will do. He will do nothing and remain quietly slaving away in the cannerys, fields, and orchards during the summers and starving the rest of the years, or, he can analyze his situation carefully and decide that he will act. He will organize to bring about a coordinated and sustained assault on the system that oppresses him until it crumbles and disintegrates so that it will never again be able to oppress people—any people. We have nothing now, it is impossible to have less and we can contribute, not only to our own liberation, but to the liberation of all the poor.

Effective action is that which cannot be undone by the Establishment, simply because it doesn't know how to deal with it. It is action that is outside the system's economic control. For example: If we educate the barrio through our own efforts (in order to mobilize la raza) the system can't deal with it, if only because we don't speak the same language. It doesn't pay us, IT can't fire us. Then the barrio (la raza) can become an independent political force imbued with its own ideology and dedicated to Chicano Liberation. We can set up our own community services of mutual aid and protection. When a chicano needs help all he has to do is to ask his neighbors and the community will respond to his need. As barrio unity increases chicano power will become a reality. Chicanos will not be brainwashed or intimidated.

El Partido de Leberacion Chicana can then represent la raza in the struggle to regain our land and establish a chicano economic base independent of the U. S. system. We will be able to staff our own schools, run our own industries, and, most important, continue to live the choice way.

The U. S. has systematically excluded the chicano, it has not provided him with the tools necessary to be a part of the economy, preferring to keep us enslaved to the rural agricultural economy, while industrialized

---

* Excerpted from Miguel Hernandez, *La Hormiga,* September 12, 1968.

America drowns itself in its stinking wealth. It has enticed us to enter with token offers and opportunities, deluding the tio tacos so they think like gringos and parrot the cliches like "working your way up," etc., but the chicanos know he can get along better without the U. S. The young aggressive chicano youth is not blind: YANKEE GO HOME! The U. S. must accept the fact that we will be free. . . . Tio Sam, entiendes?

What Do You Think?

1. Are there similarities between the Mexican-American and Black Panther solutions?
2. Why might ethnic groups not wish to give up their culture and adopt middle class white values?

5. "THEY DO NOT BUILD—THEY DEMOLISH" *

To many, rugged individualism characterized by hard work is the solution. Vice President Agnew explains "what it's all about." How might a black militant respond to the following excerpts?

Look around you and you may notice that every one here is a leader —and that each leader present has worked his way to the top. If you'll observe, the ready-mix, instantaneous type of leader is not present. The circuit-riding, Hanoi-visiting type of leader is missing from this assembly. The caterwauling, riot-inciting, burning-America-down type of leader is conspicuous by his absence. That is no accident, ladies and gentlemen, it is just good planning. And in the vernacular of today— "That's what it's all about, baby."

Some weeks ago, a reckless stranger to this city carrying the credentials of a well-known civil-rights organization characterized the Baltimore police as "enemies of the black man." Some of you here, to your eternal credit, quickly condemned this demogogic proclamation. You condemned it because you recognized immediately that it was an attempt to undermine lawful authority—the authority with which you hold your leadership position. You spoke against it because you knew it was false and was uttered to attract attention and inflame it.

When you, who courageously slapped hard at irresponsibility, acted, you did more for civil rights than you realize. But when white leaders

---

* Spiro T. Agnew, "They Do Not Build—They Demolish," *The National Observer,* August 19, 1968.

openly complimented you for your objective, courageous action, you immediately encountered a storm of censure from parts of the Negro community. The criticism was born of a perverted concept of race loyalty and inflamed by the type of leader whom [sic] I earlier mentioned is not here today.

It is deplorable and a sign of sickness in our society that the lunatic fringes of the black and white communities speak with wide publicity while we, the moderates, remain continuously mute. I cannot believe that the only alternative to white racism is black racism.

Somewhere the objectives of the civil rights movement have been obscured in a surge of emotional oversimplification. Somewhere the goal of equal opportunity has been replaced by the goal of instantaneous economic equality. This country does not guarantee that every man will be successful but only that he will have an equal opportunity to achieve success. I readily admit that this equal opportunity has not always been present for Negroes. That it is still not totally present for Negroes. But I say that we have come a long way. And I say that the road we have trodden is built with the sweat of the Roy Wilkenses and the Whitney Youngs—with the spiritual leadership of Dr. Martin Luther King—and not with violence.

Tell me one constructive achievement that has flowed from the madness of the twin priests of violence, Stokely Carmichael and Rap Brown. They do not build—they demolish. They are agents of destruction and they will surely destroy us if we do not repudiate them and their philosophies—along with the white racists such as Joseph Carroll and Connie Lynch—the American Nazi Party, the John Birchers, and their fellow travelers.

What Do You Think?

1. Some say that comments like the above represent the white backlash. State why you agree or disagree with Vice President Agnew's position.
2. What might result if a white backlash were to become general throughout the United States?

6. THE AFL-CIO MAKES SUGGESTIONS *

The reading that follows is excerpted from the civil rights plank of the AFL-CIO program for America, presented in 1968 to the platform committees of the two main political parties.

---

* Excerpted from the 1968 AFL-CIO Platform Proposals.

While much has been done in eliminating discrimination, the achievement of equal opportunity and the results which follow from it require more than civil rights laws and their implementation. For example, the right to equal service in a restaurant, hotel, or any other public accommodation is of great importance to the dignity of an individual, but the enjoyment of that right is limited by the ability to pay one's way. The latter is not taken care of by civil rights legislation. Unemployment or employment at low wages is no less a limiting factor if the cause is not discrimination but just lack of enough jobs or lack of skill necessary for the ones that may exist.

School integration is only part of the problem of adequate education opportunities. Lack of decent housing can exist without discrimination in its sale or rental. Indeed, the problems of discrimination and prejudice only compound (though quite seriously) problems of crisis proportions in our cities. These are accentuated by a steady migration from those fleeing lack of opportunities in the rural areas of the South. The new immigrants enter our already overcrowded cities unprepared to deal with the new problems they face.

The answer lies not in retreat or in reducing the kinds of social programs that have contributed to progress but in greater and more effective efforts. This is no time to abandon the struggle for equality and opportunity. It is no time to repudiate Dr. Martin Luther King's dream of a better America to be achieved by nonviolent means.

We must wipe out slum ghettos by building adequate housing for all without discrimination in its sale or rental. We must achieve and sustain full employment at decent wages with opportunities for training and advancement. We must aid schools and school systems to provide quality education while we continue the effort to end segregation *de facto* and *de jure*. We must cope with the other problems of our urban centers so that we can end the slums and their frustrations that are the tinder boxes of riots and the breeding grounds of crime and delinquency.

Nor can the government do this alone. Its efforts are necessary but not sufficient. We need and commend those efforts of business and labor which are expanding opportunities for minority group workers and youth, both by complying with nondiscriminatory requirements of the law and by going beyond them in taking voluntary affirmative actions.

We endorse the efforts of the National Alliance of Businessmen in leading companies to recruit workers who normally would not apply or be qualified for jobs. We call attention to actions by unions in developing training and outreach programs to bring opportunities to minority group youth and adults who would not normally apply or qualify for a variety of skilled and semi-skilled jobs. . . .

The struggle for civil rights requires new economic and social momentum. It is not only possible but necessary to complete the job of ending discrimination and eliminating prejudice. But a new assault on the more complex social problems that will lead to the complete elimination of poverty and deprivation must be given the highest priority on the nation's agenda.

Parallel with this effort there must be adequate appropriations to insure prompt, effective, and complete enforcement of the great civil rights legislation of the 1960s.

Violent and divisive cries on the right and the left must be rejected. Our goal must remain a truly democratic integrated society with opportunity for all as well as equality before the law.

What Do You Think?

1. Do you approve of hiring practices that favor less-qualified people from minority groups over the qualified workers who normally apply? Explain.
2. The AFL-CIO calls its platform proposals "practical solutions to the grave problems that now confront the nation." What specific programs would you suggest after having read this article?

ACTIVITIES FOR INVOLVEMENT

1. Below are listed three criteria which are often used in defining a social revolution:
   a. Large groups of people have become alienated from the existing political, economic, or social order.
   b. Meaningful communication is no longer possible between the alienated and the established order.
   c. Traditional attitudes and values are being redefined and in many cases discarded by large groups of people both within and outside of the established order.

Break the class into several four- to five-man groups to determine whether any of the readings in the previous chapters in the book would support these conclusions. Try to find any other examples that may have recently occurred in your community or throughout the country. Then hold a class discussion on the question: "Is the United States undergoing a social revolution today?"

2. Listed below are several solutions which have been suggested as ways of dealing with the problems of prejudice and discrimination in the United States:
   a. Change the attitudes of most people through education—specifically by providing courses in minority history and culture in schools, elementary through college.
   b. Send all minority peoples out of the country and back to their country of ancestral origin.
   c. Create a separate state for all minority groups.

    d. Increase the pressures on minority individuals to accept the standards of the white middle class.

    e. Create a number of on-the-job training programs in businesses throughout the country in order to upgrade the skills of minority individuals.

    f. Establish a government loan program specifically geared to loaning money to minority group individuals who set up private businesses in minority areas.

    g. Pass more laws outlawing prejudice and discrimination.

Rate each of these solutions as to whether you feel they are truly workable solutions, only partial solutions to the problems, or not solutions at all. If any are unacceptable or unworkable, modify them accordingly. Which, if any, would be endorsed by minority groups? Explain.

    3.   The Supreme Court of the United States has been severely criticized by some for its decision in the 1954 case of *Brown vs. Board of Education.* Prepare an oral report to give to the class describing the intent of the decision and what have been the results of the decision to date. A recent article in the *Atlantic Monthly* has suggested that this decision was unjust since it would throw large numbers of educationally and culturally different minority children into classes to compete with more educationally advantaged white children. Hold a class discussion on the merits of this view. How would you rebut it?

    4.   Many middle-class whites have argued that militancy on the part of many minority groups is destroying much of what goodwill previously existed between them and minority groups. This has resulted in what has frequently been referred to as "white backlash." Due to this "white backlash," many whites who previously supported minority groups are doing so no more. Interview your parents and other adults in your community to see whether or not they would agree that this is happening. What per cent agree? Do any of the suggested solutions in Activity 2 promote this "white backlash"? If so, how? Would it be possible that white backlash could be prevented? How?

    5.   Prepare a final written report in which you explain what you feel to be the most serious factor contributing to prejudice and discrimination in the United States, the greatest cost, and what you believe is the most practical solution.

BIBLIOGRAPHY
For Further Study

Books

BEAL, MERRILL D. · *I Will Fight No More Forever: Chief Joseph and the Nez Perce* · Seattle, Wash.: Univ. of Washington Press, 1963.

BISQYER, MAURICE · *Challenge and Encounter Behind the Scenes in the Struggle for Jewish Survival* · New York, N. Y.: Crown, 1967.

BONTEMPS, ARNA · *Story of the Negro* · New York, N. Y.: Alfred A. Knopf, 1955.

CLARK, KENNETH B. · *Dark Ghetto* · New York, N. Y.: Harper & Row, 1965.

CLEAVER, ELDRIDGE · *Soul on Ice* · New York, N. Y.: McGraw-Hill, 1968.

COLMAN, HILA · *The Girl From Puerto Rico* · New York, N. Y.: William Morrow and Company, 1961.

DOUGLASS, FREDERICK · *Life and Times of Frederick Douglass* · New York, N. Y.: Thomas Y. Crowell Company, 1966. (also in paperback)

FRANKLIN, JOHN HOPE · *From Slavery to Freedom: A History of American Negroes* · New York, N. Y.: Alfred A. Knopf, 1964.

GOODMAN, MARY E. · *Race Awareness in Young Children* · New York, N. Y.: Collier Books, 1964.

GORDAN, ALBERT · *Jews in Suburbia* · Boston, Mass.: Beacon Press, 1959.

GREELEY, ANDREW · *Religion and Career* · New York, N. Y.: Sheed and Ward, 1963.

HILBERG, RAUL · *The Destruction of the European Jews* · Quadrangle Books, 1961.

HUGHES, LANGSTON, and MILTON MELTZER · *A Pictorial History of the Negro in America* · New York, N. Y.: Crown Publishers, 1965.

HUGHES, EVERETT C., and EDGAR T. THOMPSON, (eds.) · *Race: Individual and Collective Behavior* · Glencoe, Ill.: The Free Press, 1958.

KATZ, WILLIAM L. · *Eyewitness: The Negro in American History* · New York, N. Y.: Pitman Publishing Company, 1967. (also in paperback)

KENNEDY, JOHN F. · *A Nation of Immigrants* · New York, N. Y.: Harper & Row, 1964.

KRAMER, JUDITH, and SEYMOUR LEVENTMAN · *Children of the Golden Ghetto* · New Haven, Conn.: Yale Univ. Press, 1961.

MANNIX, DANIEL P., and MALCOLM COWLEY · *Black Cargoes: A History of the Atlantic, 1518–1865 Slave Trade* · New York, N. Y.: Viking Press, 1962.

MONTAGU, ASHLEY · *Man's Most Dangerous Myth: The Fallacy of Race* · 4th Ed., Cleveland and New York, World Publishing Co., 1964.

MCNICKLE, D'ARCY · *Indians and Other Americans* · New York, N. Y.: Harper & Row, 1959.

SHERMAN, BEZALEL · *The Jew Within American Society* · Wayne State Univ. Press, 1961.

SKLARE, MARSHALL · *The Jews* · New York, N. Y.: The Free Press, 1958.

SKLARE, MARSHALL, (ed.) · *The Jews: Social Patterns of An American Group,* · Glencoe, Ill.: The Free Press, 1960.

STEMBER, CHARLES · *Education and Attitude Change* · Institute of Human Relations Press, 1961.

THOMAS, PIRI · *Down These Mean Streets* · New York, N. Y.: Alfred A. Knopf, 1967.

VANDER ZANDEN, JAMES W. · *American Minority Relations* · New York, N. Y.: The Ronald Press Co., 1963.

WAKEFIELD, DAN · *Island in the City: The World of Spanish Harlem* · Boston, Mass.: Houghton Mifflin and Co., 1959.

Paperback Books

ALLPORT, GORDON W. · *ABC's of Scapegoating* · New York, N. Y.: Anti-Defamation League, 1959.

ALLPORT, GORDON W · *The Nature of Prejudice* · Boston, Mass.: Beacon Press, 1954.

BALDWIN, JAMES · *The Fire Next Time* · New York, N. Y.: Dell, 1964.

BARDOLPH, RICHARD · *The Negro Vanguard* · New York, N. Y.: Vintage Books, 1961.

BEMMETT, LERONE, JR. · *Before the Mayflower, A History of the Negro in America, 1619–1964*. Baltimore, Md.: Penguin Books, 1966.

BENEDICT, RUTH · *Patterns of Culture* · Baltimore, Md.: Penguin Books, 1947.

BRODERICK, FRANCIS L., and AUGUST MEIER, (eds.) · *Negro Protest Thought In the Twentieth Century* · New York, N. Y.: Bobbs, Merrill, 1965.

CLARK, KENNETH B. · *Prejudice and Your Child* · 2nd Ed., Boston, Mass.: Beacon Press, 1963.

COSER, LEWIS · *The Functions of Social Conflict* · New York, N. Y.: The Free Press, 1964.

ELLISON, RALPH · *The Invisible Man* · New York, N. Y.: New American Library, 1963.

GITTLER, JOSEPH B. · *Understanding Minority Groups* · New York, N. Y.: John Wiley & Sons, 1964.

JAVITS, JACOB K. · *Discrimination: U. S. A.* · New York, N. Y.: Washington Square Press, 1962.

KING, MARTIN LUTHER JR. · *Why We Can't Wait* · New York, N. Y.: Signet, 1968.

LIGHTFOOT, CLAUD · *Ghetto Revolt to Black Liberation* · New York, N. Y.: International Publishing Co., 1968.

MONTAGU, ASHLEY, (ed.) · *The Concept of Race* · New York, N. Y.: The Free Press, 1964.

QUARLES, BENJAMIN · *The Negro in the Making of America* · New York, N. Y.: Collier Books, 1964.

RAAB, EARL and SEYMOUR LIPSET · *Prejudice and Society* · New York, N. Y.: Anti-Defamation League, 1959.

Report of the National Advisory Commission on Civil Disorders · New York, N. Y.: Bantam Books, 1968.

ROSE, ARNOLD · *The Negro in America* · New York, N. Y.: Harper & Row, 1964.

SEXTON, PATRICIA · *Spanish Harlem* · New York, N. Y.: Harper & Row, 1965.

SILBERMAN, CHARLES · *Crisis in Black and White* · New York, N. Y.: Random House, 1964.

VAN TIL, WILLIAM · *Prejudiced, How People Get That Way* · New York, N. Y.: Anti-Defamation League, 1960.

YOUNG, WHITNEY · *To Be Equal* · New York, N. Y.: McGraw-Hill, 1966.

YINGER, MILTON · *Anti-Semitism: A Case Study in Prejudice and Discrimination* New York, N. Y.: Anti-Defamation League, 1964.

Articles

BARMETTE, AUBREY · "The Black Muslims Are a Fraud," *Saturday Evening Post,* February 27, 1965.

BRACELAND, F. J., and M. STOCK · "Deep Roots of Prejudice," *Catholic World,* November, 1963.

CLEAVER, ELDRIDGE · "A Letter from Jail," *Ramparts,* June 15, 1968.

DANZIG, D. · "Rightists, Racists, and Separatists: A White Bloc in the Making," *Commentary,* August, 1964.

GOLDBERG, P. · "Are Women Prejudiced Against Women?" *Trans-action,* April, 1968.

HOBSON, J. W. · "Speaking Out: Uncle Sam Is a Bigot," *Saturday Evening Post,* April 20, 1968.

KOCHMAN, T. · "Rapping in the Black Ghetto," *Trans-action,* February, 1969.

KLEIN, D. · "How Much of a Man's World Is It?" *Seventeen,* November, 1967.

KNEBEL, FLETCHER · "Police in Crisis," *Look,* February 6, 1968.

MACK, R. W. · "Negro Opposition to Black Extremism," *Saturday Review,* May 4, 1968.

MCINTYRE, J. · "Public Fear and Private Withdrawal; Public Attitudes," *Current,* February, 1968.

SHEERIN, J. B. · "Catholic Anti-Semites," *Catholic World,* July, 1966.

"The Unforgiving," *Newsweek,* May 22, 1966.

TYACK, D. · "Catholic Powers, Black Power, and the Schools," *Education Digest,* February 4, 1968.

WHEELER, H. · "Moral Equivalents for Riots," *Saturday Review,* April 27, 1968.

Films

The Chosen People (30 min; ADL *) · One of a series on prejudice sponsored by the National Council of Catholic Men, this film is a sensitive discussion of the problem of anti-Semitism.

Day in the Night of Jonathan Mole (32 min; Oregon State A/V) · The problem of prejudice and the fallacies on which it thrives. A fantasy built around a courtroom trial testing a new law intended to restrict employment to people of "pure" racial origin.

Detached Americans (33 min; Carousel) · Problems and explanations concerning apathy in the U. S. today.

Everybody's Prejudiced (21 min; Oregon State A/V) · A comparison between the kinds of prejudices employed by most people and the unreasoning prejudices of a bigot.

Exploding the Myths of Prejudice (color; Human Relations Series; Warren Schloat Productions, Inc.) · Discusses the myths and misconceptions underlying racial prejudice, pointing out that prejudices are the learned results of an individual's social environment.

Growing Up Black (color; Human Relations Series; Warren Schloat Productions, Inc.) · Reveals the realities of black childhood in our society.

Harlem Crusader (29 min; EBF) · Social worker in Spanish Harlem.

Heritage (10 min; ADL) · An animated color cartoon on human rights, moral values, and the relationship between rights and responsibilities.

The High Wall (32 min; ADL) · The case study of a bigot, and how he got that way.

Make Way For Youth (22 min; ADL) · How teenagers shelved racial prejudice in favor of cooperation in recreational and civic projects.

Minorities Have Made America Great (Parts 1 and 2) (color; Human Relations Series; Warren Schloat Productions, Inc.) · Each filmstrip reveals the many problems faced by a particular minority group and recounts its contributions to American life. Part 1 includes Negroes, Jews, Germans, and Irish; Part 2 includes American Indians, Orientals, Puerto Ricans, and Mexican-Americans.

---

* Anti-Defamation League.

One Potato Two Potato (54 min; Trans-World) · Study of a mixed marriage.

Picture in Your Mind (16 min; color, ADL) · Traces the roots of prejudice, and how and why man continues to have prejudices and fears.

Rush Toward Freedom (color; Human Relations Series; Warren Schloat Productions, Inc.) · Five filmstrips show dramatic social revolution of the civil rights movement. Discusses violence, confrontation, direct action.

Sit-In (54 min; Oregon State A/V) · The Nashville lunch counter sit-ins are covered along with the preparations that went into the entire protest movement.

To Find A Home (28 min; ADL) · A Negro family tries to rent an apartment in a Northern city and meets with rejection.

To Live Together (30 min; ADL) · Tells about the experiences and difficulties encountered by a group of children at an interracial summer camp.

The Tenement (30 min; ADL) · Life in a black ghetto in Chicago.

They Have Overcome (color; Human Relations Series; Warren Schloat Productions, Inc.) · Award-winning filmstrips documenting the achievements of five prominent Negroes in the face of enormous odds (Gordon Parks, Claude Brown, Dr. James Comer, Dr. Dorothy Brown, Charles Lloyd).

The Toymaker (15 min; color, ADL) · Two hand puppets are friends until they discover they are "different."

The Victims (50 min; B/W) · Dr. Benjamin Spock, author, teacher, and pediatrician, diagnoses the causes of prejudice in children. Through a series of interviews, Dr. Spock demonstrates that adults are the carriers of prejudice, but they also have the power to cure.

Voyage to America (12 min; B/W) · The contributions made by each immigrant group to the building of our country. This film was produced for the United States Department of Commerce.

Walk in My Shoes (42 min; B/W) · A documentary in the "Close-Up" series exploring the innermost feelings of the Negro as he reacts to prejudice and discrimination in America.

Willie Catches On (24 min; Oregon State A/V) · Influences of teachers, parents, and peers in developing prejudice in the mind of a boy.

Records

Buffy Sainte Marie, *Many a Mile*. Vanguard.

CORE Freedom Marchers. Dauntless.

Freedom Songs: Selma. Folkways.

Human Rights. E. Roosevelt. Folkways.

Nashville Sit-in Story. Folkways.

On the War Path. Folkways.

Pete Seeger, *Songs of Struggle and Protest*. Folkways.

Six Million Accuse—Eichmann. United Artists.

West Side Story. Columbia.

Tapes

Captain Richard Pratt (H328; A/V Center, Univ. of Michigan) · Promotes the idea of education for the Indian.

Future of American Race Relations (#14A; A/V Instruction, Coliseum 131, Corvallis, Oregon) · By Thomas Pettigrew.

Huron (H181; A/V Center, Univ. of Michigan) · Sad story of the Hurons from colonial times to the present.

The Indian Today (H101; A/V Center, Univ. of Michigan) · Typical Indians comment upon their day to day activities.

New Frontiers of Human Freedom (15 min ea; 1.00; A/V Instruction, Coliseum 131, Corvallis, Oregon) · Fourteen tapes on discrimination and intolerance. Excellent series.

Race and Education (#12A; A/V Instruction, Coliseum 131, Corvallis, Oregon) · Some research findings by Thomas Pettigrew.

We Are Americans: Our International Heritage, 1965–1966 Series. For Slow Learners. (A/V Instruction, Coliseum 131, Corvallis, Oregon) · An exploration of America's international heritage. Each program devoted to the contributions of an individual ethnic group represented among Americans today. #14 is not available.

1. First Americans
2. Italy
3. England
4. Veterans' Day
5. Hungary
6. Thanksgiving
7. Scotland
8. Sweden
9. Germany
10. Christmas
11. Spain
12. Greece
13. Norway
15. China
16. Africa
17. Armenia
18. France
19. Poland
20. Netherlands
21. Ireland
22. Russia
23. Japan
24. Latin America
25. Belgium
26. Hawaii